The Pact

Goodbye, Past. Hello, Love!

CHARLES J. ORLANDO

one room press
Los Angeles, CA

This book is an original publication of
One Room Press
A division of Loft 327, Inc.
816 S Broadway, Los Angeles, CA 90014
oneroompress.com

ORP Paperback Edition 2015
10 9 8 7 6 5 4 3 2 1

1. Interpersonal Relations   2. Self-Esteem
3. Consciousness & Thought   4. Marriage & Adult Relationships

ISBN 0-6925-4238-5
ISBN-13: 978-0692542385

Cover by Saavedra Design
Printed in the United States of America

FOR DREW AND JORDAN

You kids are crazy, and are part of the driving force behind most things I do. I can't thank you enough for adding to my insane life, just by being who you are.
I love you both with all my heart.

ACKNOWLEDGEMENTS

. . . .

To those who have read my writing, written in for advice on life and love, and allowed me to touch your lives: I'm honored and humbled.

My friend and business partner, Lisa Steadman: You watched this being born. Thank you so much for your support.

My friend and confidante, Melanie Gorman: Thank you for your tireless belief in my message.

CONTENTS

....

INTRODUCTION
. . . .

I've spent the last 45 years listening to men and women. Sometimes I've listened as a little brother—paying close attention to my older sisters' dating exploits. Sometimes as a pick-up artist—running with a group of players, portraying the best parts of my personality in an orchestrated effort to steal my way into many a woman's bed. Sometimes as a serial boyfriend—screwing up relationships that magically lasted past a one-night-stand. Sometimes as a husband—figuring out first-hand the issues that plague established, long-term relationships—and learning from my mistakes along the way. And sometimes as a researcher, writer, and interpersonal relations expert—hearing tales of both wonderful and broken relationships, the issues that led to their success or failure, and offering advice to hundreds of thousands of readers and fans.

In an effort to stay abreast of ever-changing times, apps, technologies, and modern-day issues, I have stayed listening—online, in-person, over the phone, via email, through friends, at speaking engagements, at book signings, and on social media. What people want and/or think they want from a relationship varies—most often starting one way at the beginning and then changing over time. Whether it's life in general or love in particular, one thing is consistent across gender, socioeconomic background, geography, profession, age, and upbringing: Everyone wants to be happy. For some, happiness is money (read: money is no longer a limitation on what they want). For others, it's giving and/or receiving love— being valued and accepted by someone else. Others are driven by a sense of accomplishment—whether it's becoming a top executive at a software company, the manager of the local shoe store, or achieving the status of a Top 100 Reviewer on Yelp. And still others are driven to start a family with their focus on building all a family requires—house, car, private schools, a playroom for the kids, barbecues and ballgames on the weekends, college tuition, and ongoing expenses ad nauseum.

From these examples, the reality is illuminated: Happiness is not only individualized, it is highly dependent on where we are at physically, mentally, financially, and spiritually in our own personal existences. Too many people falsely believe that they will achieve the "right" level of personal happiness if [insert something here]. The list is endless…

"I'll be happy…

…when I graduate."

…if I can make enough money."

…when I get promoted."

…if I can only move to a better city."

…when I'm out of debt."

…when I meet the right person."

…as soon as we get married."

…once the kids are out of the house."

…when I can cash in the IRA."

…the moment my divorce is over."

…when I can travel."

…when I retire."

Read the above statements again, because the same person—at various points in their life—spoke them. It is in reflection of these statements that life's biggest truth becomes self-evident: Happiness is not only dependent on where we are at emotionally in our own existence; it is also a journey, not a destination. The path is most often not a direct one, but instead winds, twists, changes and shifts as we travel upon it. Once we arrive at the destination that we planned on, we enjoy it for a time. But then we see something on the horizon—something different that we want in addition to (or more than) what we have currently. We seek to achieve this new goal in our ceaseless quest to grow, learn, feel, and attain new knowledge and experiences—our hearts and minds set on becoming more than the sum of our proverbial parts. We want to feel. We want to connect. We want to know. We want to smile. We want to feel fulfilled. We want to be loved. We want to feel complete in this incomplete world.

These behaviors are part of what drive us as human beings. But too often, we look outside for what we need to address inside. Happiness, as they say, is an inside job, but so many people don't completely internalize this notion until later in life. Those who are young (read: below 40) don't know what they don't know—and after 40 we *still don't!* We try to formulate our life plan in our teens (perhaps earlier), but by the time we get into our twenties and thirties, things have changed. We then adjust, or have already altered, what we want and where we are headed—a process that continues throughout our lives.

This constant state of adjustment is evident in our love lives. Not because of *who* we love, but because of *how* we love—and how we value and receive love—changes as we learn more about ourselves, and what we want from a relationship. We choose partners based on our experiences and our internalization of what we do, feel, and see—starting in our childhood, guiding us through our teen years, and on to adulthood. We reflect on the good and bad of what we've seen—from our parents' relationship to our own—and formulate what feels good and normal when it comes to love.

But there is a big difference between "normal" and "good". For some, the feeling of normal is actually just familiarity—which is to say if someone finds themselves in relationship after relationship that is filled with slights, resentment, abuse, or indifference it will start to *feel normal.* For people in this situation, a good relationship is something that remains elusive and/or unattainable. They end up convincing themselves that all men or all women "are the same", meaning they are going to be treated poorly no matter who they choose to love. The saddest part is that we all want and deserve love and happiness. Unfortunately, many people forget to look in the most obvious place: inside themselves.

Part of my personal and professional journey has included connecting and interacting with thousands of people, and it's been an amazing gift. As I write this, I have just over 13,000 requests for advice in my inbox (and, yes, I reply to as many as I can daily). I've responded to thousands of people over the past years, people who are smart, brave, longing, searching, and wondering about how they can better relate to their partners. They want to keep things connected. They want to understand the *whys* of their partner's behavior. And they have many questions about life and love…

"Why didn't he call?"

"How can I get her to listen to me?"

"Why does he care more about his friends than me?"

"Does he love me, or is he just using me for sex?"

"Why won't he commit?"

"What happened to our sex life?"

"Why doesn't she value what I do for our family?"

"How can I get him to love me like he used to?"

These questions all have a central theme: Something is wrong with their partner or their partner's behavior. Perhaps that's true. But in digging deeper into these questions and discussing the issues, situations like these can become much clearer. There are myriad reasons for how and why people relate (or don't relate). Not only is it the proverbial "two sides to every story", but there's also a third side: The experiences, issues, and baggage that everyone brings to their relationships. By far, these are the most influential—and potentially damaging—issues when it comes to how we relate in dating, marriage, and friendships. The challenge: We don't know what we don't know. We don't recognize the deeply rooted issues that we cart around with us—from relationship to relationship—and how they impact what we do, how we think, and how we interpret what is said and done by those we love.

We're blocked. Things we feel—but don't have a firm grip on—block us. Issues from our past relationships, our family of origin, our interactions at work… All these things and more have a direct impact on our happiness—with others as well as within ourselves. We struggle to understand and make changes, but oftentimes end up circling around the same issues in vain, never solving them; we just reenact situations and experiences with new people. To alter these patterns, we need to look at the *real issues*—not just the symptoms we experience in our day-to-day lives, but the actual issues that are blocking us from receiving the love we want.

These are the reasons I wrote *The Pact*. To make positive change, we need to address the real issues that lie beneath the symptoms. We need to acknowledge and work through what's blocking us, and the only way that works is to let our guard down and face things head-on. No ego. No fear, and no denial; just the plain, direct, unadulterated truth staring us in the face. Once the truth is apparent, we can't pretend any longer; we can only solve the issues. If we don't, we are now active participants in our own unhappiness.

In the thousands of sessions I've held with people around the world, there are 10 dominant issues that stop us from giving and receiving the love we want. These are Love Blocks, and they are inside all of us—stopping us from getting the love we want and deserve, and causing so many of us look past the right person and stay in bad patterns with those who won't add to our happiness. The only way to get past these issues is to embrace them. In essence, you have to go through it to get to it.

In the pages that follow, all 10 Love Blocks are detailed out for examination, along with methods, exercises and techniques to address them—hopefully dispelling them. Note that these blocks are challenging to work with, tapping into core issues we have all experienced in our lives. As such, these pages are easy to read, but the exercises and methods will take time and repeated effort to put into practice.

After reading through a Love Block, you will be asked to take a Pact. This pact is a mental agreement that is meant to shift your thinking, allowing you to take control of the issue that is blocking you, and guiding you with techniques that will start the process of putting issues behind you in a meaningful way.

As you read and apply what's discussed, please remember you are in control of you. Sometimes life deals us a rough hand. And while you can't change the hand you're dealt, you can certainly choose how you will play it.

THE PACT

LOVE BLOCK #1

· · · · · · · · · ·

THE PAST

"As long as you make an identity for yourself out of pain, you cannot be free of it." —*Eckhart Tolle*

The past is how many people define who they are. Some define it through their successes, their careers, or their kids. Others summarize their selves by embracing their pain—prior relationships turned bad, bad childhood experiences, absent parents, or other negative issues from their lives. But here's the thing: Good or bad, success or failure, love or hate, the things that we experience and/or happen to us don't define us. They can add to our life's experience. They can help or hinder us in how we see things, they can make us view things in new or unusual ways, but they don't define us unless we choose to take on the label.

We all tend to embrace labels—short, tall, gay, straight, smart, brunette, fat, thin, divorced, impossible, single, dumb, annoying, clingy, unattractive, brilliant, under-achiever, parent, sibling, child, immature, dumped, wife, old, bald, crazy, not good enough, hopeless, irresistible. Some of these things do make up who we are (no one can really change your height, you can dye your hair but your true hair color doesn't go away, once a parent always a parent), but they are only a part of you.

Personal Account:

At 5'4" (163cm), it goes without saying that I'm not the tallest guy on the planet, and for much of my childhood I was branded "The Short Guy". It gave me quite a complex. But here's the thing: It didn't give me a complex. I gave it the power to affect me. I chose to buy into the label—to take it on as the definition of me, who I was and what I had to offer the outside world. As a result, it became all I had to offer myself. I decided that I couldn't do this or that because I was "too short". I was only "allowed" to do certain things, as those are the things short people are "allowed" to do. This was my script. I kept it and lived it every day … until my sophomore year in high school.

I wanted to go out for the basketball team in high school. I had been playing baseball for years (and made two all-star teams as third baseman), and my height was never a problem. But basketball was going to be different. Everyone out there was over six feet tall. They were taller, bigger, stronger, and more experienced than I. But I really wanted to play.

The question: Was I tall enough? Meaning: was my Short Guy label actually who I was, or was I something more? I thought about it—honestly, openly, and critically looking at myself, my weaknesses, and my Short Guy label. Could I dunk? No, but I would work on my outside shooting and score without needing to dunk. Was I big enough to physically power by these behemoths— some of whom were 12 inches taller than me? No, but I was fast so I would work on my dribbling and beat them with agility.

With this fast analysis, I changed my entire outlook on what was possible. Am I tall enough? Who cares? The new question quickly became: HOW can I play, instead of SHOULD I play. And my answer was straightforward: Embrace my weaknesses. Take them in. Acknowledge them. Accept them. They are a part of me, but they do not define me. They are a piece of me, but they do not encapsulate me.

You may feel that you have a variety of labels. That's okay; we all feel that way. But no matter what they are—positive or negative—they only have power if you choose to let them define the entirety of you. *You are not your labels. You are more.*

From an early age, we are conditioned by society to just accept the norms as the way things are, and there is no changing it. Boys hit girls in grade school "because they like them"; girls need to "act like a lady"; strong boys don't cry—only wimps cry; girls need to be "good girls" so a boy will want them; boys who sleep with many women are studs, but the girls they sleep with are whores, and so on. Through these forced behavioral archetypes, we are predestined to adhere to what the world around us views as "normal". And it's not that straying outside the lines isn't allowed, it's that many of us are so conditioned to blend into the pack we don't see that we can choose something different for ourselves.

Maybe you were a poor student in school. Does that mean you will *always* be a poor student? Perhaps you were abused or molested as a child. Is that because you deserved it, and now that's *what you should expect?* Maybe you were bullied. Does that now mean *you are the world's punching bag* for mental and/or physical intimidation and abuse?

We take on labels from our relationships: The Cheated-On. The Divorcée. The Unlovable. The Never-To-Be-Married. The Failure. These are just some of the things many of us decide we are when a relationship goes sour. We look at what happened to us. We feel the ugliness. We experience the loss. We hate what happened and, after we get past the anger, we end up settling on a very sad realization: There is something wrong with who we are, and that's why these bad things happen. It translates to some very negative internal thoughts and statements that are based on bad labels:

- Unworthy: "I end up with the losers because that's what I deserve."
- Invisible: "I'm never going to find the right person for me."
- Embittered Victim: "Everyone cheats. It's just a matter of time."
- Valueless: "I won't find anyone better than my ex."
- Cynic: "There's no such thing as love."
- Self-Hatred: "I'm too fat to be loved."
- With Baggage: "I'm divorced with two kids. Who would want me now?"
- Unlovable: "It doesn't matter. I'm just unlovable."
- Past Their Prime: "I'm too old. Everyone wants a 22-year-old with a bangin' body."

I wish I were making these labels and statements up, but they (and hundreds of others) are uttered by so many people, and the negativity is deafening. And it's not that these people want to be negative. They are just in so much pain that it manifests itself in ways that "prove" that they are to blame for what has happened.

There are things you're able to change, and there are things you're not able to change. Either way, you can choose what you do with your experiences. The past cannot be undone, un-experienced, or ignored. Bells cannot be unrung. But what you have gone through can make for a better future.

Your internal dialogue is a large part of what drives you. It's your personal script that creates your experiences, and guides you towards what's next for you, for life, and for love. Regardless of the messages that are coming from the outside world, two simple truths are guiding you:

1. Every day you are growing. You can choose in which direction you grow, but you will grow. You can feed your positivity or your negativity.

2. Every day you can choose. Your thoughts about and outlook on life, love, and everything around you are within your control. You can choose how you feel and how you act and react to what happens.

WHAT YOU AREN'T ABLE TO CHANGE
YOU CAN EMBRACE.

WHAT YOU AREN'T ABLE TO EMBRACE
YOU CAN RELEASE.

If you are reliving the past—positive or negative—you are not in the present ... and not headed towards a future filled with what you want. Some things you aren't able to change. You won't be able alter the past, and there's no way to undo things that have hurt you. But what you have experienced has helped mold you into the person you are today. The real question is: What are you going to do with it?

As I did in basketball, you can embrace your (real or perceived) weaknesses, your shortcomings, and your bad experiences. They can be channeled into strength, into courage, and into focus. Things happen to all of us. We experience pain and loss. We don't get precisely what we want or need from the universe. To grow and to learn new ways is part of the human experience. It's not about getting past things, it's about moving through them—to acknowledge them, deal with them, and then use the experience to make your life better.

Letting go of people, ideas, expectations, desires, bad habits, false beliefs and unhealthy relationship... Every day, every moment presents an opportunity to create ourselves anew, to shrug off the baggage of the past, open ourselves up to the possibility of the moment and take action to create an incredible future.

TAKE THE PACT OF ACCEPTANCE

It's not all your fault, but it's up to you to change it now. It's time to acknowledge the issues that have led you to feeling inadequate, complacent, and/or upset with how life is shaping up for you. Recapture your power and make the following agreements with yourself:

- Embrace what you are able to do, and channel it into strength.
- Release what is out of your control.
- Accept your life as a series of experiences—experiences that present you with situations to learn and grow from.

Easier said than done? You bet... That's why it's a process, not a destination.

EXERCISES

Over the next 7-10 days, please complete the following activities. Don't convince yourself that you can do these things "later" or "some other time". If you want to make changes, do these things starting now—and then continue doing them.

THE "I CAN'T" LIST. Spend some time sitting quietly and make a list of the things you can't do. At the top, print clearly and in large letters: I CAN'T. And then start the list. And *everything* goes on this list: can't find the right job, can't get your partner to listen, can't find time to go to the gym, can't find love, can't get kids to listen, can't get up on time—everything. Embrace all the negativity you can muster. Make it complete, using as much time and as many pieces of paper as you wish. When you're finished, fold it in half and take it outside. It is time for a funeral. I Can't has officially died, and you need to bury it. You can get an old shoebox and bury him, or choose to cremate him (observing local laws and safety) but I Can't has died, and we need to pay our respects. Before covering the shoebox or setting the paper ablaze, please take a moment to reflect on the following eulogy—reading it aloud or to yourself:

> *"Here lies I Can't. He was a part of my life for so long, a semi-permanent part of my language, my*

existence, and my interactions with others. I'm sad to see him go, but he was sick and is now in a better place. He is survived by his brother I Can, and his twin sisters I Will and I'm Going To Right Away. I'm excited to continue the journey with them."

Bury or burn your list. I Can't has died, and you'll need to start rephrasing your words and discussions to acknowledge it. You might not be able to do something, or you might not know how, but it isn't because you *can't*.

REFLECT ON AND EMBRACE YOUR DISAPPOINTMENT AND BITTERNESS. When things don't go our way, it's normal to be upset. Give yourself some time to feel all the anger and disappointment that stems from things that have caused you pain, but put a hard limit on the time you will spend, as this is your chance to feel it. Now, consider the following:

- Consider dealing with your past. If you have people from your past that have hurt you, consider communicating how you feel to release your past. Note that you can't control how they respond; you can only control how you express yourself.

- Face your own accountability. When we're upset, we tend to focus on what someone else did that was wrong. This takes your power and control and gives it away. When you focus on yourself—what you could have done better—you are taking control of you. This causes empowerment to flourish and embitterment to dissipate.

CHANGE YOUR MINDSET BY TAKING ACTION.

- Kill off negative thoughts. Wear a rubber band on your wrist and snap it when you start delving into things that are negative from your past. This serves as a physical reminder to stay in the present, and release what you are not able to control.

- Learn a new skill. Instead of dwelling on things you've never learned or are unable to accomplish, pick something you've always wanted to learn—and then start learning it. Guitar, cooking, a language… it's up to you.

- Replace your past. If you find yourself thinking, "No one will ever love me," allow the feeling in. Then move on to a different thought about your life that is positive. Think about what you have done, what you are doing, and what you have accomplished.

- Manifest your present every day. Every morning, before you get out of bed, ask yourself three questions—and then answer them—aloud: 1) What am I grateful for? 2) What do I have to look forward to today? 3) How can I make someone else's day incredible?

ADVANCED WORK

With your new mindset, you should branch out.

- If you don't already, pledge to start a short workout regimen every morning for 10 minutes. Taking a walk around your neighborhood, stretching, or sit-ups are a great place to start. Do it before anyone else wakes up. All it takes is setting your alarm a few minutes earlier, but the mental and physical benefits are tremendous.

- Having trouble releasing a past relationship? Take control of the situation and write your thoughts in a letter. It doesn't matter if you send it; what matters is getting it out on paper. Be honest, hateful, angry, confused... whatever. Express yourself and get your bottled-up feelings out so they lose their grip on your life.

- In the evenings, take a few minutes to reflect on your day in your own space. Think about the following: 1) There are no failures. You learn from everything you do. 2) You deserve great love. 3) Be open to new ideas, people, and situations, which will enhance your joy and happiness.

Dispel and discard your labels, embrace your challenges, and release your past. You will be empowered to change your view of what's around you and move on to life and love that is great—for you and those around you. Happiness and positivity start from within you, and you are now on your way.

THE PACT

. . . .

SELF-WORTH

"We cannot think of being acceptable to others until we have first proven acceptable to ourselves." — *Malcolm X*

Self-worth is defined as "the sense of one's own worth as a person." How we establish our own self-worth can be influenced by and linked to a variety of factors: home environment, experiences with friends and close relatives, influential authority figures, trusted mentors, and many others that come in and out of our lives. But the keyword here is critical: *influenced.* We have the choice about what we choose to accept—from what others think of us to what we believe about ourselves. The hard part is taking control of what gets in, how we internalize it, and what we do to self-correct if we find ourselves thinking negatively about our worth.

Worth is about *value*, and *self*-worth is based on how you feel about *yourself.* What you believe about yourself can and will dictate what you allow into your life—the behavior and treatment by others, the partners you chose, the employment you accept, the list is virtually endless. Are you *worthy* of that great job? *Valuable* enough to have an incredible relationship? *Important* enough for your kids to listen and follow your rules? *Loved* enough for your significant other to treat you as an equal? If you don't think you are worthy then you are destined to be disappointed and hurt. You will assign value to yourself by what others say about you, to you, and/or how they treat you, and you are then looking to them for validation, acceptance, and their assessment of your worth.

Self-*Worth* or Self-*Esteem*?

If you are feeling negatively about yourself—or allow others to treat you poorly—you more than likely need to build up your self-esteem. Self-worth and self-esteem are often used interchangeably, but they are not identical. According to Merriam-Webster elf-esteem is defined as "confidence in one's own worth or abilities". Therefore, worth vs. esteem can be defined as internal vs. external. As such, self-esteem is only one side of the equation, and is most often affected by external sources—friends, family, successes, failures, environment, and more. It is susceptible to forces outside of you—forces that shift on a dime. In psychology, assigning your value this way is called Contingent Self-Esteem, and is largely dependent on how you feel about yourself in reflection of what the world sees. In essence, you are assigning your own value based on your reflection as seen by others—their perception of the way you look, think, and act.

Self-worth, on the other hand, is about how you feel about you—regardless of outside influences or fluctuations in your own successes and failures. You understand that you are human and make mistakes, screw thinks up, and do things that might not be in your/others' best interests, but you forgive yourself and move on. Your mistakes, errors, and misgivings don't define you; they create a better you because you learn and let go of what was so you can get to what will be.

Self-esteem and self-worth are complementary, and have a symbiotic relationship, feeding each other with the positives and negatives of life, which is where things can go awry. Self-esteem without self-worth builds a person with a false external projection of themselves. They are a shell that can be easily crushed by outside influences, comments, opinions, and perceptions. Self-esteem that is built on a foundation of positive self-worth is not only genuine, it is formidable and virtually unbreakable—an indestructible fortress.

The biggest problem is that outside influences have a nasty habit of changing how we feel about ourselves.

Example From Society:

The Stock Market Crash of 1929 affected thousands of people— business professionals, financial advisors, families, and corporations. Companies closed, and people lost their savings and security overnight. For many in the financial world, they had become one with their fortunes. In essence, their self-esteem had been built on the perception of what others saw: cars, houses, bank accounts, and the cash in their wallets. When the money disappeared and these rich professionals were left with just themselves as people—without the benefit of material objects to boost their fragile self-esteem—many of them became chronically depressed, hurt those they loved out of anger and fear, and even committed suicide. Their entire vision of their own value was built on what others saw instead of what they saw, believed, and felt about themselves. Like a hollowed-out eggshell, they had a hardened appearance, but it was a façade—a façade that was crushed under the weight of their own perceptions of their lack of value. No money meant that they were worthless and, without worth, they didn't see their purpose in life anymore.

Self-worth and self-esteem profoundly affect our relationships, as well, and nowhere is that more evident than in bad relationships. Let's start at the beginning.

It's a common lament: "You can't choose who you love." Not only is this a statement of victimhood—predicated on the thought that we are just fated to love someone, regardless of how they treat us—it's also completely false. Love and attraction don't just "happen". We *select* others. We *choose* potential partners and mates based on a combination of what we like and what we feel we are worth. Think about it: If you feel valuable to *you*, you would never allow yourself to stay around someone who treats you poorly. You would recognize that you aren't being treated with the respect and dignity that you are *worth*. But in bad relationships—where partners might act abusively, be emotionally unavailable, or fundamentally unable to fulfill critical needs of ours—that is precisely what happens, and failure is virtually predetermined right from the beginning. Red flags are ignored, poor behavior and treatment is allowed (and in many cases, encouraged), and all the issues that should be glaringly obvious are excused. Selecting someone who will never fulfill our needs or treat us with value creates a Cycle of Worthlessness.

The Cycle of Worthlessness—Defined

When we choose someone who is unable to fulfill our core needs, we do so for a variety of reasons.

Sometimes, they treat us well at the beginning and then things suddenly change for the worst. With other partners, they might feel familiar/comfortable because of our past bad relationships. Or they might fit perfectly for some of our core needs, but don't address other areas in the relationship. Regardless of the red flags and the issues we see (consciously or unconsciously), we assign our *personal value* to this wrong relationship/partner. We give them what they want, fulfill their needs, love them, adore them, support them but it is not returned. And it leaves us wondering why. *"What wrong with me?"* we ask ourselves. *"If I were doing things right, wouldn't they treat me better?"*

Their actions (or lack thereof) translate to us as "you're not worth it," so our self-esteem suffers. But because we value this wrong person's view of us more than our own—and we think if we give more they will come around to see what they have been doing wrong—we put more effort into them and the relationship, believing that if we are truly valuable, they will see it and they will treat us better. But it has the opposite effect. They pull back further and continue not giving us what we want, which drops our self-esteem lower. The lower our self-esteem gets—and the more often these dynamics are experienced—the more our perception of our self-worth is negatively affected. We begin to believe that we aren't worthy of good treatment, that there is something wrong with us, that we aren't worth the effort. We become desperate for validation, so either: 1) We act out or fight with them, because negative attention and validation is at least something; or 2) As desperation is an unattractive quality, they break-up with us (or cheat, or ignore us further), which "proves" to us that we are actually not worthy of anything good; that we "deserved it". And when the relationship ends we repeat the cycle— because it's familiar, and ties directly to our current sense of self-worth.

A reality check: If you base your self-worth on what others think then you are basing your value solely on their acceptance of you. This is a fatal error that causes you to falsely believe that if they don't accept you then you have no worth. This is the fundamental reason why people stay in abusive or damaging relationships too long: They feel that they *can't* leave, because whatever worth they feel they have (or hope to gain) will be left behind if they vacate the relationship. For them, it's easier to stay in a bad relationship rather than doing the hard (and healthy) work of rebuilding a true sense of self-worth within themselves.

Perhaps the bad stuff is easier to believe, but that is only because you have already bought into someone else's thoughts. Their opinion of you is just that: an opinion. Just because they say it doesn't make it true. You are the ultimate decider of who you are, what you stand for, what you believe, and what you will accept. You don't have to run with the herd; you can lead yourself, for yourself. What you think about you is 100 times more important than what others think. You don't have to accept their view as fact, and you aren't required to believe what they say. You have your own internal voice of value, and *that* is the voice that counts. And this is why your self-worth is so important. You own your worth. It's yours. Your positive self-worth will trump someone else's view of you every time… if you choose.

Example From Society:

In the 1980s, Johnny Carson was still host of The Tonight Show. He was in his prime, and his nightly guests were energetic and fun. One night, Joan Rivers came on right after his monologue (which was hilarious). She came through the curtain with the music playing, shook Johnny's hand, and took her seat on the chair opposite him on the set. He welcomed her with a boisterous, "Joan, it's great to have you here. Glad to have you back!" To which Joan replied, "Thanks, Johnny. [pause] You know… you look tired." Johnny didn't miss a beat. She had barely gotten the words out of her mouth when Johnny replied, "No, I don't. I look great and I feel great. So, Joan… Tell me what's going on with you. How are things?"

Joan Rivers' view had no power on Johnny Carson's view of himself. It didn't matter if it were true or false. It was rendered powerless because Carson's sense of self-worth wasn't dependent on others' thoughts or observations. He knew who he was, what his value was, and why he was important to himself. His bottom line was straightforward: "Don't tell me what or who I am; I already know."

So why does this happen? How do we end up thinking so lowly of ourselves that we aren't worth good things, great love, and proper treatment? Quite simply: We buy the bullshit. We believe what others say and accept it as Gospel, and then we run with it. And I get it. Sometimes, after years of emotional slights at the hands of our family of origin and our past relationships and friendships, it's only human to start thinking, *Wow. Okay, this is the [insert number here] person/relationship that has treated me this way. There must be something wrong with me.*

This is how self-esteem translates to self-worth, and if you think that something is "wrong with you", you would be half-right, but not for the reason you think. It's not that there is something wrong with *you*, it's that there is something wrong with:

1. You valuing someone else's view of you more than your own.

2. Your selection process of friends and relationships.

3. You assigning your worth to the notion of "If they change, then I am valuable."

Once you start down the path of negative self-worth, it can be hard to break out of it. One negative viewpoint leads to another, until all you feel is self-doubt. This is why—for many people—one bad relationship leads to many. People in these situations think they have many bad relationships in a row. But, as I've stated, this is a matter of self-worth, not chance or luck. As such, they haven't had many bad relationships; they've had *one* bad relationship *many times*. Until they change their view of themselves, the pattern will repeat.

The worst part: By selecting partners who are bad, people in these situations are automatically not selecting partners who might be good for them—by default. The good partners aren't even given a chance, because the wrong relationship is being chased over and over again.

The only way through this is a hard realization: You have to see things for what they are—how you are sabotaging yourself, and how you are creating and bolstering a negative pattern. It's not that you want or mean to end up in dissatisfying situations, but you are *actively choosing* that path… And awareness is the first step to change.

What's needed is a mind shift, a belief that you *are* worthy. Naysayers don't own you. They don't control your view of you. You are in charge of you and your belief in yourself. But here's the rub: By reading these words, you have created awareness for yourself. If you *choose* to stay on a path of negativity, self-doubt, and unhappiness, it's a choice. You can only be a victim if you are unaware. But by reading this you *are* aware, and with awareness comes accountability to change your outlook.

TAKE THE PACT OF SELF-WORTH

Never let anyone else's bullshit convince you that you aren't worthy of love and happiness. You are. Anyone who tells you otherwise is on a separate path, and it is not your responsibility to sink to their level. You have a responsibility to yourself, for yourself, to get the most you can out of life and love. Don't settle for unhappiness because you falsely believe you are unworthy.

You. Are. Worthy. When you know it, everyone else will recognize it also. If they don't, you won't even notice, as they won't fit into your life's plan.

EXERCISES

Over the next 7-10 days, please complete the following activities. Don't convince yourself that you can do these things tomorrow. "Tomorrow" is just a code word for "never". If you want to make changes, start doing these things right now.

ASSESS THE STATE OF YOUR SELF-WORTH. Answer the following questions using the following scale: Strongly Agree, Agree, Disagree, or Strongly Disagree

1. I am a person of worth.

2. I have a number of good qualities.

3. I feel I can be successful in what I put my mind towards accomplishing.

4. I am able to do things as well as most other people.

5. I have pride in many things in my life.

6. I like me.

7. Looking at my life, I am satisfied with where things are for me.

8. I demand respect from those with whom I interact.

9. I believe that I'm useful.

10. Generally, I'm a positive person.

Calculate your score as follows:

Strongly Agree = 4
Agree = 3
Disagree = 2
Strongly Disagree = 1

Scores between 23 and 34 are within the normal range. Scores 22 and below suggest low self-worth.

STRIVE FOR SMALL VICTORIES. When people start down the path of self-improvement, they often reach for large goals. The problem is, if that goal isn't reached—as is often the case—they relapse into thinking that they are "still a failure". Of course, that's not the case; their expectations were simply too high. Smaller goals are achievable and they build your sense of accomplishment. With victories, you feel good and successful. Start small with basic things: pay a bill one week early; fill your gas tank when it's half full instead of waiting until it's empty; set a goal to do 10 push-ups every morning for a week. Small successes allow you to plan and push for larger plans.

- Make one daily goal and write it down (or put it on the to-do list app on your phone). Check it off when completed. In the evenings, create a new goal for the next day.

- Make two weekly goals and write them down (or put them on the to-do list app on your phone). Monitor your progress as you check in on your daily goals.

REDEFINE YOUR SELF-IMAGE. If you are basing your assessment on a past version of yourself, you are setting yourself up for failure. Just because you could bench press 200lbs in college doesn't mean you can do that at 45 years old. Reassess your current self by making a Strengths and Weaknesses Checklist.

Draw a vertical line down the middle of a piece of paper. On the top-left, write "Strength." On the top-right, write "Weaknesses." In each column, write 10 things—things you excel at, and things you need to work on. If you have challenges thinking of 10 things, revisit to what friends, family and co-workers have told you. By creating this list, you will not only see what needs work, but what you are incredibly good at. This gives you the opportunity to see the value you bring to yourself and those around you, as well as areas you can develop as you grow into the New You. Now, select one weakness from your list to work on weekly.

DEMAND RESPECT FROM THOSE AROUND YOU. What you allow is what will continue. If you grant others permission to walk on you, you will eventually become a doormat. You are worth more than abusive statements, disrespect, passive-aggressive behavior, or being ignored or disregarded. If someone refuses to treat you with value and respect, you need to tell them how you feel. If their behavior doesn't change, you will likely need to consider changing your relationships status with that person. Easier said than done? Perhaps. But you are valuable and worthy… You just have to know it before things will change.

- Abusive Relationships: Given the state of dynamics in emotionally or physically abusive relationships, it can be dangerous to suddenly alter your behavior. You could put yourself in harm's way. Instead of a direct confrontation, seek out advice from a trusted professional, friend, family member, member of the clergy, counselor, or law enforcement officer. You are valuable and need to remove yourself from the situation—but smartly.

- Marriage, Kids, And Finances: If you are in a marriage with children and they are treating you with disrespect and zero value, it's not so simple to just leave. Counseling is a good start. If that fails to change the behavior, you might have other decisions to make. Seek out the assistance of a counselor or licensed therapist to assist you in planning the next version of your life. You are important to YOU and if you are in a situation where they don't value you—and won't alter their behavior—it's likely time for change.

ALLOW YOUR NEGATIVITY AND DOUBT TO COME IT... THEN: KILL IT. When shifting your mindset, it's normal to have old thoughts creep in and create doubt in your newfound positive outlook. Don't sweat it. Let those thoughts come in and then revisit the Strengths list (#3 above) to re-bolster your self-worth.

Above all, release your idea of perfection. No one is perfect. We strive for greatness, but we make mistakes along the way. Such is life. You win some, and you learn some.

ADVANCED WORK

- Choose one of your Weaknesses from the Strength and Weaknesses List you made earlier this week. Open your calendar and set aside some time to address this issue. You can think about it, learn new things about it, or simply decide that it's not important to you at this time and cross it off. Whatever the case, *take action*.

- For three days, find four people every day and compliment them on something. Two should be friends or family, the other two should be people you don't know or whom you've just met. Document what happens.

- For 24 hours, don't compare a single thing you do to anyone else's activities, accomplishments or failures. Live in your skin, and yours alone without sizing yourself up against other people.

THE PACT

LOVE BLOCK #3
. . . .

CONFIDENCE

"Confidence is the ability to feel beautiful without needing someone to tell you." —Mandy Hale

Belief in oneself is one of the biggest roadblocks facing people today. Confidence can be emotionally (and sometimes physically) beaten out of us at an early age—and that lack of self-assurance can follow us for our lives. The tricky thing is that confidence shows itself in a wide variety of ways. It represents itself in what we say, what we do, how we interact with others, and—most importantly—how we view ourselves.

Confidence is in our words, our body language, the way we walk and stand, our eye contact... everything. If you are comfortable and confident, it shows. No matter what we do, our current level of confidence is ever-present and is affected by our feelings of self-worth and self-esteem.

Think back and remember a time when you felt really in the moment. What you said clicked, you were completely connected with what you were doing and to whom you were speaking—and you could feel it. Those moments are almost electric; they crackle in the air. You are just in the zone, you know it, and your confidence level builds on itself as the better you feel about you the better you perform. But if you're off then the reverse is also true. Low confidence sabotages even the most talented of us. You can't seem to get anything right. You can't find the words, whatever you do never really connects with a good/solid outcome, and you end up in an unsure place and unable to mention things that might make a difference and change things.

Feelings of confidence require one major shift in our thinking: no self-rejection. We have been taught that we need to achieve some level of goodness that will be acceptable... of perfection that needs to constantly be strived toward... that who we are, what we believe, what we say, what we look like, how we dress, the way we act, and the things we have are not good enough.

STOP IT!

We are all growing and learning. We are all imperfect. We are all screwing things up, making mistakes, and finding new ways to inadvertently add challenges to our lives. Getting past them to some untold, unknown destination isn't important. What *is* important is what you learn through the process. What matters is your journey. What matters is that you are incredible, not *in spite* of your flaws, but *because* of them.

Getting rid of our expectation of self-perfection might sound contrary to the effective building of confidence. It sounds "wrong" because we have been taught through our lives that being everything to everyone that matters will result in our acceptance by others. We have been programmed that striving for perfection is what we all do and will result in us being happy. We see this "perfection" in every magazine we read, every celebrity photo we view, every relationship we hear is "so great", every pic we see of others posting their oh-so-perfect lives on Facebook or Instagram, and we want to feel accepted the way we see others being happy and accepted. These perceptions affect our confidence level, which, in turn, affects our level of satisfaction and happiness.

KEY QUESTION: How happy and confident would you be if you stopped comparing yourself to others' lives and experiences? I'll tell you: You would push to learn more and be the best version of you that you could. Without focusing on a useless comparison with others you wouldn't feel inadequate, and thus your confidence would remain high because you would be proud of you and your own growth. But we don't do that. We try to keep up with the Joneses. We read others' social media updates and feel that we don't have enough, aren't doing the right things, and are somehow unacceptable. We chase a false image of perfection that we have attached to various external sources, but what we don't see happening is that we are killing our confidence—silently and extremely effectively. We view ourselves as unacceptable in our current state, and we strive not to be better, but to be perfect. And "when we get there"—to that level of right, of perfect—we will be happy. By pushing to become an external idea of perfection, we inadvertently reject that which makes us *us*, therefore undermining our confidence.

Personal Account:

In high school, I played baseball competitively. I was a really good third baseman. (Hear that confidence?) Actually, I was one of the best in the league. In the final tournament, I was hoping I was in the running to make the All-Star Team, and I knew I had a shot. My team won the championship and I was sure I was in—but I wasn't. Many members of my team (and other teams) went on to play in the All-Star Game... just not me. Was I disappointed? Yes, however we had just won the league championship. Was "coming in as the second-best third baseman" a blow to my confidence? No way. I had made critical, key plays to help get my team to the championship, and I helped us win. So, while it was normal for me to be disappointed, it didn't brand me as "second-best". And it is here that a critical life lesson is dished out: What others believe is their perspective, but it doesn't define you. Confidence is a reflection of what you know about you.

However you define happiness—pleasure, contentment, satisfaction, cheerfulness, merriment, gaiety, joy, joyfulness, joviality, jollity, glee, delight, good spirits, lightheartedness, well-being, enjoyment; exuberance, exhilaration, elation, ecstasy, jubilation, rapture, bliss, blissfulness, euphoria, transports of delight—it's already in you… You just have to accept you for who you are… the great, the learning, the mistakes, the excellence, the faults, the pain, the joy, the sorrow, the amazingness that makes you *you*. And *you* are the source of your confidence.

The challenge that arises when we enter a relationship is that to connect and live with someone else requires compromise. Compromise is a good thing. It allows us to bend, learn new things, and put another's needs in-line with our own. However, many times compromise gives way to sacrifice, and that's when the trouble can start. Some sacrifice is natural, even acted on with pleasure. Raising children, shifting careers, budgeting money can all require some level of sacrifice. The dictionary defines sacrifice as "to give up something important of value for the sake of other considerations," which is to say that the "other considerations" are more important. In essence, we are talking about trade-offs and prioritization—both of which are active, conscious choices. The sacrifice I'm discussing isn't so straightforward. It happens slowly, over time. Little sacrifices give way to larger ones, and before you know it you are sacrificing your core needs—what you want; what you believe; what you need. You might start thinking that what you need is wrong, that you don't deserve it, or that you aren't able to ask for it. This reflects on your self-value and comes out as a lack of confidence. And therein lies the vicious cycle: No self-worth leads to self-doubt leads to a lack of confidence leads to no self-worth. And when we lose the confidence in ourselves, not only do we think what we need is wrong, but we also don't have the confidence to ask for or change it.

The Key To Self-Worth and Lasting Confidence Is To Maintain Your Individuality

Couples that invest in each other and build their lives together do stay together. But what people often forget is that couples are also made up of individual men and women with their own wants, needs, dreams, aspirations and desires that exist outside of the relationship. Developing or keeping your sense of self-confidence in a relationship may prove to be difficult if you already have a low sense of self-esteem or have been hurt in previous relationships (head back to Week Two to get working on that if you are still struggling), but building and maintaining a solid sense of self-confidence will not only positively affect you and your life, it will impact the lives of those around you. It will grant you better physical and mental health, increase your ability to handle stress and problems that life might throw at you, and allow you to tackle new things without second guessing yourself.

TAKE THE PACT OF CONFIDENCE

Never give up your individuality. People who put everything into their relationships and leave nothing for themselves are setting themselves up for failure. Maintain your own life, interests, and friendships.. and then share things back to your relationship and with your significant other. There are some great people out there, but you won't find them if you ignore the warning signs, sacrifice your confidence and individuality, and settle for second-best. Maintain your confidence, and you will quickly eliminate those who don't really want you for the long haul... And you'll do it without taking a single hit to your self-esteem.

EXERCISES

STAND NAKED. Look at yourself in the mirror—no clothes. What you will see is a human with great physical and mental qualities, some things that need to be worked on, and some things that will, unfortunately, never change. That is what we all look like and guess what... This is who you are. That reflection represents the outward representation of what you have been granted this time around. Get to a place of acceptance of the YOU of you.

LIVE IN GRATITUDE FROM THE MOMENT YOU WAKE UP. Every morning, look up at the ceiling (not your phone on the nightstand, just the ceiling) and take a moment to be grateful, and do it before you even get out of bed. There are SO many things to be grateful for, and if you let go of the things that crowd your mind, you will think of them easily.

LIVE YOUR CONFIDENCE. We have a tendency to let things slip. Every day for the next week, take care of you: shave, do your hair and/or makeup, dress nicely, and walk with a slight swagger. (Hey, you look good!)

IMPROVE YOUR HEALTH

- After rising, perform 10 each of push-ups, sit-ups, and jumping jacks, every morning, right next to your bed. Get your blood flowing. (Can't do 10? Try five. Still too many? Start with two and work your way up.)

- Eat breakfast every day. (Don't argue that you don't have time in the morning; just wake up about 15 minutes earlier.)

REFLECT ON THE POSITIVE. Take 30 minutes every afternoon to sit outside and just reflect on your day. No kids, pets, significant others, nothing. Think about your day and review something you are proud of, a risk you took, a skill you learned, a person you helped, or an opportunity you received.

10 KEYS TO BUILDING
LASTING CONFIDENCE IN LIFE AND LOVE

Read these every day, and pay attention to how they play out in your everyday life.

1. See yourself as an individual—now and always. Whether you are in a relationship or not, you are always YOU. Love doesn't complete you. It might complement you, but it doesn't complete what isn't already there. You need to know how to be good with you before you can be with someone else.

2. Believe in your value and act on it. Your confidence is something that will manifest itself in every action you make and intention you set. To set your confidence in motion, do things that make you feel good! Whether you start hitting the gym or get your hair cut/done, learn something you have never done before, or start a new hobby, acting with intention and confidence breeds you feeling good about you … and if you are feeling good about you, you will bring that back to those around you.

3. Don't stay in a bad relationship. Too often, people get stuck trying to make things better or right, believing if they do more then the relationship will work. But a confident person knows their worth, and

would never stay in a relationship with someone who doesn't value, appreciate and respect them. A confident person has no fear in leaving a relationship where they are shown they are not valued. They voice their needs—and if things don't change, they move on.

4. Develop and maintain your own interests. Having interests and doing things that don't include your partner isn't just normal, it's critical for you to maintain a sense of self.

5. Don't overanalyze what people say, and don't automatically accept it as the truth. Just because someone gives you feedback, criticism or their opinion doesn't make it real; it is just their perspective. Listening to their view is great, but make sure you think it through before you accept it as reality.

6. Sometimes things just end, and that doesn't make it your fault. Relationships—romantic or platonic—sometimes just wrap up. People might not be a match, they might have changed their views or wants, or they might grow apart. A relationship ending doesn't necessarily mean that someone did something wrong, it might just mean that things

have changed too drastically to continue on their current path. It's not about "fault"; it's about how life shifts.

7. Trust in yourself. There are no guarantees that you will make the "right" decision every time. None of us have a crystal ball. But if you've taken a look at the options, make a decision and then trust your judgment. Will you be right every time? Of course not, but you need to go with your gut instincts and not second-guess your decisions. Make a choice and follow it through.

8. Set boundaries and keep them. Healthy boundaries and self-worth and confidence go together. By maintaining strong boundaries of what you will allow for and around you, you are stating that you are a priority... you are important... you have needs that need to be addressed. And you won't be guilt-tripped or manipulated into putting yourself in a situation where you need to sell your integrity or needs just to maintain a relationship.

9. Don't require reassurance to serve as validation. Everyone loves a compliment or to be accepted, but it shouldn't be a necessity. Having confidence means that you know you have value, you feel that you are

loved and you are clear that you are lovable... And a relationship doesn't need to fill the void in your ego or help you bury your insecurities.

10. Accept responsibility. Being confident means that you recognize that you are in charge of YOU. You aren't a victim of anyone else's actions, as you can see that you always have a choice to accept what the circumstances are, change the situation or leave.

ADVANCED WORK

- Say hello. For the next 24 hours, smile and greet every person who makes eye contact with you. It doesn't have to be a long interaction (or creepy). Just smile, say hello, and move on.

- Pay attention to your posture. Stand tall, sit tall, and really feel the room you are in. (Others will feel your presence, too!)

THE PACT

LOVE BLOCK #4

. . . .

SELF-DOUBT

"If you hear a voice within you say you cannot paint, then by all means paint and that voice will be silenced." —*Vincent van Gogh*

Confidence is critical. It's the self-assurance that gives you the internal strength to feel good about you and all that you are. However, when you put your needs out for someone else to examine and evaluate, you are allowing them to see that you are vulnerable. You are stating (or silently implying) that you need them to fulfill something you can't get yourself or build internally. You are asking for something that matters to you and by saying it, you are giving them the opportunity to satisfy what you want... or not. The "or not" is the scariest part. After all, if they say or imply that they aren't interested in fulfilling your wants and needs, it can translate to ugly things, both for the relationship as well as for you personally. Statements like, "I'm not worth it to them," or "I should have never told them," or "Forget it," might creep in and begin to work their destructive capabilities on your self-worth. But they can also become powerful defense mechanisms allowing you to rationalize staying quiet under the guise of "staying safe". After all, what they don't know can't hurt you.

But it's *not* safe. In truth, by trying to convince yourself to stay quiet and not voice what you want, you are lying to yourself. By pretending that what you want isn't important or needed, you talk yourself out of getting your needs fulfilled. You end up doubting whether your needs matter at all. You end up blaming others—including your partner—for not knowing what you want. Resentment builds, anger bubbles up to the surface… and before you know it, you are unhappy that your needs aren't being met and dissatisfied in your relationship.

No one wants to be judged. Putting your wants, needs, and desires out there means that you are opening yourself up to be evaluated and judged. Holding back your thoughts and feelings leads to bad places: jealousy, insecurity, clinginess, and other damaging behaviors. And no matter how much someone loves you, acting this way will eventually drive people away, and will prevent you from finding and keeping the love you want and deserve.

Are you harboring self-doubt? Pay close attention to things you say (to yourself and others) as well as what you think.

- "I'm not sure."
- "What I want isn't important."
- "I don't need it, I just want it."
- "Maybe I was wrong."
- "I don't feel up to the task."
- "Never mind."
- And my personal favorite: "It's easier said than done."

All of these phrases are things someone says when they are subconsciously de-prioritizing what matters to them most and talking themselves out of happiness. You tell yourself that what you want or need isn't important or possible—or maybe it will take a lot of effort. As a practice, the more you de-prioritize your happiness, the less you believe you deserve happiness, and the less happy you become. This becomes a self-fulfilling prophesy for unhappiness.

As soon as we say or think anything similar to any of those phrases, we should attempt to identify the source. (Note: These and other expressions don't always indicate self-doubt, but we need to check it out.)

DO NOT UNDERESTIMATE
THE DESTRUCTIVE POWER OF DOUBT

Doubt is an expression of insecurity; it can bore itself into our very core and undermine our strongest beliefs. Many times, doubt comes from a past experience where we believed the wrong person, were hurt by who we thought was the right person, or by being treated poorly by someone we incorrectly deemed important. These experiences probably (and unfortunately) taught us four bad lessons: 1) Never let your guard down; 2) Don't allow people to get too close; 3) What people say isn't what they really mean (or are doing); and 4) What is important to me isn't really important to anyone else, so I won't talk about it.

Your Past Can Become Your Present

Maybe you were cheated on. Maybe they played you financially. Maybe they lied over and over. Whatever the case, you took them at their word and it ended up being bullshit. And once you found out, you not only felt stupid (and you spun and spun on that thought for a LONG time), but you also vowed that it would never happen again—ever.

Infidelity

Maybe you doubt yourself and your value because someone cheated on you. You might have thought you let it go, but it's still there … ever-present … and it rears its ugly head in your current relationships—friendships, romantic relationships, even work/professional situations. It comes out as insecurity. You wonder all the time if they are telling the truth. You quiz and question them about where they are, what they do, and why they are doing it— sometimes even laying little word traps in your conversations to see if they are lying or not. These insecurities end up causing strain on your relationship, and they can't deal with your controlling/possessive/insecure behavior… So they break things off (or you do, because you are convinced they are lying).

THE HARSH TRUTH: YOU DON'T REALLY DOUBT WHAT THEY SAY… YOU DOUBT YOUR ABILITY TO SPOT DISHONESTY.

The saddest part of this situation is also the simplest: What happened in your past relationship still has control of you, and for good reason. Your Bullshit-O-Meter didn't go off when it should have, and now you think everyone has an ulterior motive or is looking to pull one over on you. But here's your Wake-Up Call: They didn't lie or cheat on you because of who YOU are. They acted that way because of who THEY are NOT. They weren't worthy of the treasure that is you, and that's not your fault.

Wrong Relationships

Perhaps you stayed too long in the wrong relationship, hoping that you would be seen as worthy and valuable. You stayed and stayed and stayed... And every day they showed you that you were optional in their life, or that your wants and needs didn't matter, that they would call you when they got around to it.

YOU ARE NOT AN OPTION. YOU
ARE IMPORTANT. STOP DOUBTING
WHAT YOU WANT AND NEED.

The real question is: Why aren't you speaking up and saying that what you want is important and then sticking to your guns?

Those with low self-esteem often look externally for someone who can validate them and validate what they want out of life and love as important. However, by not having a strong sense of worth, they end up finding the same unfulfilling relationship over and over again, most times with a partner who doesn't value them and doesn't care about anything other than themselves. This leads them to one of two places: 1) An endless cycle of hurtful relationships, ending in bitterness that "all men/women are the same: selfish, egotistical jerks"; or 2) They improve their selection criteria and the quality of their partners, but their self-doubt translates into relationship insecurities. As such, they push a good partner away because they are conditioned to look for problems instead of just putting their needs out honestly and openly.

Leave the past in the past and stop giving your insecurities power. Love is like sand in your hand, the tighter you hold it the more it slips through your fingers. Either trust them or let them go. Scary? You bet, but sometimes you have to let go so you can hold on.

Self-Doubt Due To Self-Sacrifice

Perhaps you put your needs on the back burner because "It's what's needed right now," or "It's what my family needs," or "I need to be supportive of what is important to them." All those statements are fantastic and they allow for great intimacy, sharing and connection with your partner, but such action not only needs to be valued, it needs to be reciprocated. YOUR needs are just as valid and valuable as theirs. It's not your job to make sure everyone's life works at the expense of your own. You are important.

Many times, people don't discuss what they really want from the other person for one reason: fear of rejection. For many, it's easier (and safer) to do without needs getting met rather than risk the other person not wanting to fulfill them. But that is where some of the real trouble can start.

The Danger of Unspoken Expectations

Firstly, let's get something super clear: It's NORMAL to have expectations in your relationships. Having no expectations means you have no standards on how others are allowed to treat you. It's normal and good to have rules on what you expect from others, as well as boundaries on what you will accept and what you will not.

But if you doubt that your expectations are important—to yourself or to your partner—you might clam up and keep them to yourself. If you do, you are laying the groundwork for not only dissatisfaction, but for a potential break-up.

THE SEED OF RESENTMENT IS PLANTED THE MOMENT YOU CHOOSE NOT TO SAY WHAT IS IMPORTANT TO YOU.

You have to tell your partner what matters to you. You have to say it. You have to put your needs out there. It doesn't matter whether or not they can fulfill them completely. It doesn't even matter if they care about what you want. What DOES matter is that you say it, that you mean it, and that you feel in your heart that it's important to you. Put your needs out there and then you'll have a chance to see their reaction and can gauge their response.

Could they reject you? Yes. Could it not matter to them? Yes. Could you be disappointed? Of course. But by not saying anything, you are virtually guaranteeing that your needs don't matter and that your partner has no chance to fulfill your needs and make what you want count.

Don't assume the worst. Study after study shows that people drastically underestimate how positively their partners see them and want to help them. However, if they don't want to help you and your needs don't matter to them you have a different choice to make, don't you? After all, you matter to you, right?

TAKE THE PACT OF FORTITUDE

No one wants to feel inadequate. No one wants to be judged. No one wants to feel that they aren't important. But you start with valuing YOU, and with that value comes the ability to voice what matters and have it heard. It matters to YOU, so speak up!

FOUR STEPS TO OVERCOMING SELF-DOUBT

1. LOOK AT YOUR DOUBT FOR WHAT IT IS... AND ACCEPT IT. You cannot conquer anything unless you are willing to look at it for what it is, in all its challenge and ugliness. To overcome self-doubt and step into your power, not only do you need to

acknowledge its existence, you need to accept that it is a part of you at this time. Self-doubt can be sneaky and pretend to be other positive attributes in your relationship: support, maintaining peace, sacrifice or compromise, putting yourself last because "you are just that giving"—all these things are red flags. If you suspect that it exists, you need to pull it into the light so it can be dealt with.

2. EXAMINE AND DRILL-DOWN. Spend some time looking at your relationships—past and present. What's happened in your relationships (romantic, work, familial, or friendships) to cause you to stop voicing your thoughts, feelings, wants and needs? When you analyze your feelings, stay true to what's real and not what you wish would have happened. Make a list of potential situational and/or relationship triggers that cause you to feel unsafe and then clam up.

3. LOOK FOR A PATTERN. Self-doubt likes patterns. Do you have a number of relationships that have some striking similarities with how you have felt in them, or perhaps how they ended? Are you resentful of friends, family, or past partners for how they didn't fill your needs or desires? Did you discuss what you wanted from them, or did you send hints or signals,

thinking, *If they are paying attention they will fill my needs?* Do you find the same person over and over and none of them addressed what really matters to you? All of these scenarios have the same common denominator: you. Continue your list to establish what's happened.

4. SAY WHAT YOU MEAN, AND MEAN WHAT YOU SAY. Telling someone what you want can be scary, even intimidating. The main thing that can help is to focus less on the other person and his or her reaction and more on your own clarity. Figure out what you need to say and/or how you feel and say it straight. The thing to remember is that you can't control how they react, and it's not your job to care-take them or their reaction. You are in-charge of *you*, and they are in-charge of *themselves*—which includes their reactions and emotions. Say what you need, mean it, and allow them the space to accept it or reject it—knowing that it's not a reflection of you or the validity of your requests.

From here, it's a matter of practice. If you aren't able to do this the first time out, it's not a failure. Any new skill needs to be practiced and tested. You might have a few false starts. And trying again is more than acceptable; in fact, it's required for personal success and happiness. Most importantly: Do it. If you scare yourself into never doing it, you will never develop the skills you need to communicate openly and effectively—and you will never get your needs met. You matter. When you know it, everyone else around you will know it also, or they won't stay around long as your standards will prevail.

REMINDERS

- Strive for balance. There's a difference between being aggressive and being assertive.

- Always take the opportunity to say what's on your mind. Maybe the barista at the local coffee shop got your order wrong. Tell them. Perhaps a your closest friend has been doing something that really bothers you. Speak up!

- Listen and accept feedback. Sometimes, when we start down a new path we can overcompensate. Listen to those you love and trust to gauge your newfound strength. Make sure you are dishing out the proper amount of assertion.

THE PACT

LOVE BLOCK #5

· · · · · · · · · ·

CAVING IN

*"Be who you are and say what you feel, because those who mind
don't matter, and those who matter don't mind."*
—*Bernard M. Baruch*

Everyone wants to meet that special someone. Once we feel we have, we can't get enough of them. We see how similar we are and revel in the connectedness of the new relationship. We want to introduce them to our friends, our families, and share our interests with them. But then things might shift. The friends and interests we once had start to fade away. What takes their place? "Couples' activities". We give up our own interests and start doing what they like to do, calling it "support". They might have a stronger personality, so we become intimidated and afraid of making them upset. Perhaps it's their career that pays the bills, so we justify putting our wants and needs on the back burner. Children might enter the equation so what was a couple's existence now gets convoluted with family time, and then the marriage takes a back seat. We let go of our opinions, beliefs, and desires and convince ourselves that we aren't caving in, but rather we are "keeping peace".

In any relationship there is a natural need for give and take; both individuals want separate things (or outcomes) and need to meet in the middle so everyone gets the majority of their needs met. That is what makes a successful compromise, when each side makes concessions that they are willing to accept without harboring resentment.

When involved with someone else emotionally, spiritually, physically and financially, there is an inherent need to meet in the middle to make things work well. A functional relationship demands compromise, be it about cohabitation, time, kids, chores, bills and finances, or life in general. However, many times the balance of power becomes tipped permanently in one person's direction, and before you know it one person is doing all the "compromising" and not getting what they want while the other is holding all the power in the relationship and getting anything they choose. One person "convinces" the other that their way is the "right" way, which leads to one end: the other person caving in. This is a recipe for disaster for both people and is most often terminal for a long-term relationship.

The person who caves in becomes angry and resentful. This resentment can manifest outwards—passive-aggressive behavior, rebellion, disconnection, disrespect, contempt in tone and action, or emotional outbursts—or inwards—headaches, sleeping disorders, anxiety, chronic sickness with no direct cause, stress, self-doubt, depression and, in extreme cases, suicide.

Interestingly, the person who doesn't cave in also becomes angry and resentful. Their resentment can also exhibit itself outwards—disrespect, controlling behavior, possessiveness, contempt in tone and action—or inwards—making joint decisions without consultation, hiding of key information such as finances, blatant lack of communication and, in extreme cases, mental and/or physical intimidation and abuse.

SOMEONE WHO IS WORTHY OF YOUR LOVE WILL NEVER PUT YOU IN A POSITION WHERE YOU MUST SACRIFICE YOUR DIGNITY, YOUR INTEGRITY, YOUR CORE BELIEFS OR YOUR SELF-WORTH TO BE WITH THEM.

But relationships don't start this way. After all, if we started dating someone who was a control freak who demanded that we give up everything we want on date #1 and do everything their way, the vast majority of people would roll their eyes, end the date, and move on. While sometimes the signs of these dynamics might show themselves early in the courtship process, most often this shift in relationship dynamics occurs slowly and imperceptibly over time. It happens when we release our individuality and, in that release, compromise turns to sacrifice.

When you meet someone special, it's more than natural to want to please that person. And while some compromise is necessary to a successful relationship, giving up your individuality—the stuff that makes you *you*—is not just a bad idea, it sounds the death knell for the relationship in the long-term. Giving up the things that make you who you are not only makes your individual life empty and unsatisfying, it also reduces the qualities and activities that attracted your partner to you in the first place.

IF YOU NEED SOMEONE TO
COMPLETE YOU THEN YOU DON'T HAVE
ENOUGH OF YOU TO BEGIN WITH.

The Subtle Release of Individuality

We're taught from childhood, and long into our adult lives, that we need to find someone who "completes us". We're shown by friends, family, and society that the measurement of being "worthy" is being desired by another and marrying for life. We believe the romantic comedy hype and think we need to marry our best friend, expecting them to fill all our requirements for the entirety of the relationship. And to do all these things, we convince ourselves that what's needed is sacrifice—of our wants, our beliefs, our long-term plans, our self-worth.

Subconsciously, and perhaps unintentionally, we start to let go of who we are. Some people do it because they fear losing someone they love, so they will do anything to keep the relationship. Others fear conflict or confrontation, so it's better to just do things "their way" to keep things running smoothly. And it usually starts slowly. You might begin acting differently when you're together, hiding or ignoring pieces of your personality due to your own insecurity about what they might think if they "actually knew you". Perhaps you change your hair or style of dress, your musical tastes, or your outside interests. Before long, your partner ends up falling in love with the person you've shown them, not the person you actually are. As a result, you end up dissatisfied in your relationship and your own life—resentful of how things turned out and angry at the relationship you tried to adjust yourself for in the first place.

And these changes are virtually imperceptible until later in the relationship. You might believe you are doing it because you are "growing" into a couple or that you are just changing your mind about things. But, in truth, you are releasing your core essence. You are caving in to the false pressure of what you feel is needed to keep the relationship functioning and happy. You are virtually guaranteeing that your relationship will fail. The risk: Could they leave if they discover the "real" you? Yes, that is a risk for any and all relationships. But it's better for you both to discover that you aren't a match rather than pretend you are. All pretending leads to is the false notion that you are connected to someone who isn't actually a real match for you—and you will have to keep sacrificing and caving in or the relationship won't function.

Doing activities as a couple is normal and adds to the togetherness of the pair, forms a bond. However, when "I" becomes "We" and "We" becomes only "Them", you are headed down the path of caving in.

Key Identifiers That You Are Caving (Or Have Caved) In

- You have given up your personal aspirations, dreams and goals. Everyone has their own wants, needs and desires out of life. If you are ignoring yours (or pretending that they don't matter or that you will "do it later"), you are caving in.

- You have lost contact with your friends and/or family. No one person can address all your needs. A relationship is about sharing, but it's not meant to fill 100% of your needs.

- You feel they don't respect you. If you aren't being treated as an equal (regardless of who pays the bills), the power balance is off in your relationship.

- You have no alone time. Spending time with your significant other is great, but that doesn't mean ALL your time needs to go to them. If your time is only going to them—or to serve them—or to responsibilities for a joint life (to include kids), you are sacrificing, not compromising.

- You have no outside hobbies or interests of your own. Doing your own thing and then sharing that back in your relationship is normal. If you're not, it's a red flag.

- You are being told how you are "allowed" to dress, act, or speak. This is a huge warning sign for a controlling relationship, bordering on abuse.

- You don't make decisions for yourself and/or aren't involved in decisions for the relationship. You are an equal part of your life with them. You aren't an attendee to your life or relationship. Decision-making isn't just a necessity; it's your right.

- Your personal level of happiness is dwindling or non-existent. Not happiness as a couple or parent, your happiness. If you constantly doubt yourself, questioning your thoughts and opinions, wondering what they might think or say, or are generally unhappy, you are farther down the path of self-sacrifice and caving in than you first thought.

A healthy partnership will add to your identity, bringing out sides of your personality that you never knew you had, and introduce you to things you never knew you would like... but it won't "complete" you. Be yourself. Expect your partner to love you for precisely who you are, and be prepared to love them back for who they are.

TAKE THE PACT OF INDIVIDUALITY

Getting in touch with *the you* of you—without guilt or feeling the need to apologize—is the goal of The Pact of Individuality. You should *never* lose who you are in a relationship, automatically caving in to their wants and needs.

EXERCISES

9 INDELIBLE RULES FOR MY INDIVIDUALITY

To be read every morning—aloud.

1. I don't need anyone's permission to do anything in my life. I have personal rights and am entitled to make my own choices. I realize that I might need to discuss some decisions with my partner, but I am in charge of me. If they truly love me then they will support me in the healthy things I choose for myself.

2. I will keep my own friends and stay in touch with my family. As much as we love each other, and as inseparable as we are as a couple, I will make a conscious effort to spend time apart. I love my friends and family, and I get a lot from them.

3. I will keep my outside interests and hobbies. It's good for me and for my relationship to have outside interests, and perhaps share them back with my partner. Things that bring me happiness should being my partner happiness through me.

4. I am entitled to say, "No." I don't owe anyone an automatic "Yes" answer. I have limits and boundaries, and I am entitled to hold them, even if that makes my partner (or others) unhappy or upset. I matter to me, and setting healthy limits is part of it.

5. I will stay open to new things. Part of being an individual is to see when things need to adjust in my life and in the lives of those around me. I recognize that things change and I will strive to keep an open mind.

6. I give myself permission to be wrong and make mistakes. I'm not perfect. It's what makes me human. My mistakes do not define me.

7. I might not agree, but I will listen to my partner about things in my life. I know I won't always be right—even about things that only concern me—so it's important that I listen attentively to outside views of those I love and trust. From there, I can choose if I accept their views and advice.

8. I realize that anger can be very manipulative and controlling. I will not cave in to someone's requests because I don't want them angry or disappointed. They are entitled to their feelings just as I am entitled to be me.

9. I will not let go of my dreams. I recognize that other things or activities might need to be prioritized above things that matter deeply to me, but I will choose to put them in the order I decide. I will not let go of my wants and needs—or prioritize them based on someone else's decisions—as they are what define me as a person, and I am important.

Awaken your *you* through Three Steps of Reflection

STEP ONE: Create your own life timeline. On a sheet of paper, make two columns. On the left, write down all of the major goals that you feel you have achieved and/or want to achieve. On the right, document the events in your life that have already happened and that have shaped or affected you. When life presents us challenges, those events shape our belief system and make us think and see things differently. These are the points that make us *us*.

This list is a documentation of you. The goal of this exercise isn't to feel sad or disappointed in what you have achieved or not achieved. It's about clarifying and identifying issues that might be blocking your individuality and contributing to potentially damaging behaviors like caving in. Spend some time clarifying each of the main events on the left and the details on the right. Example: Your early goal was to complete graduate school; put that on the left. But you had kids at a young age and you and/or your partner wanted you to devote your time to raising the kids; put that on the right.

STEP TWO: Review the timeline and separate your thoughts and beliefs from the thoughts and beliefs of others. Life is pretty easy to go through while on autopilot. When we're kids, we are told the roadmap for a "good life": achieve good grades, go to college, get a job, get married, have kids, believe this, ignore that. All of that is good guidance, but it's not YOU. At the end of your timeline, perform the following:

- List out at least three beliefs of yours that are based on what you've been told. Now, write what you actually think of them. Example: Maybe you've been told that children who have one stay-at-home parent have a better head start in life. Is that a core belief for you? If so, then you made your choice based on your own values.

- List how you feel about the world around you. What's good and what's bad according to you, not anyone else?

- Think about what you would change on your timeline—keeping in mind that the good and the bad have led you to precisely this moment in time. If you consider changing things, why are you changing them—for you or because you missed someone else's expectations?

- How can you achieve what you want on your timeline? Are you telling yourself it's too late? For some things, the honest truth is that it might be. After all, it's highly unlikely you can achieve a goal of becoming an Olympic ice skater if you've never had lessons and you're 35 years old. But look objectively at your timeline. What are your goals today in reflection of your life? What doesn't apply anymore?

What do you want to achieve? What can you adjust to accomplish what you want from your life?

STEP THREE: Make changes in your everyday life. Self-reliance and self-worth are the keys to individuality and not caving in. If you don't have a solid sense of self-worth, you'll listen to what others have to say all the time and be swayed by their insistence on what is appropriate.

- Start trusting your own judgment and decision-making processes, mistakes and all. We all make mistakes, but through mistakes we find ourselves growing, learning, and reaching our real selves.

- Start taking responsibility for budgeting, household matters, and planning for the future. People who lack a sense of self tend to disregard the "details" of life with a carefree attitude, believing that things will all sort themselves out. But things don't always sort themselves out. Taking responsibility pulls you back from the precipice and lets you be self-reliant and self-determined, no longer carried along by the waves of fate.

REMINDERS

- Trust yourself. You know yourself better than anyone else.

- Don't lie to yourself or try to be someone you are not. You are you, and you're great.

- Remember not to let others decide for you what you are destined to do. Their path may not be the correct path for you. What works for one person may not work for the next.

- Don't change who you are or how you act just to fit in.

- Don't over-analyze things. There is no right or wrong. If you're doing it and on the path then you're doing it right.

THE PACT

. . . .

UNCONDITIONAL LOVE

"Unconditional love can be great... provided the conditions aren't all about them. When you give unconditionally but are receiving conditionally, you are on the road to becoming a doormat."
—*Charles J. Orlando*

From early in life, we (or at least many of us) experience a form of unconditional love. As infants and young children, our parents show us unconditional love as a combination of three distinct behaviors: acceptance, understanding, and gratitude. They place no conditions on their love for us. No matter what mess we leave, what grade we achieve, or what poor choices we make, they accept us. They work tirelessly to understand us as we are and strive not to force us down a path to change. They are grateful for us. We are extensions of them. They view us as such, so in accepting us they, in effect, accept themselves.

Then … things change. We enter the real world where we discover that the people around us aren't like our parents, and, as such they aren't quite as understanding or accepting (to say the least). They have rules. They have expectations. They have boundaries. We are greeted with all these conditions and don't understand it. We think, *What happened to people just accepting me no matter what?* And it is here that the disconnection between what is learned in childhood and the reality of adulthood is revealed. We falsely believe that whatever we do is going to be accepted. And despite the continued dissatisfaction and disconnection in and with others, we think we are right in how we are, and it is they who must change and adjust. After all, we are more than acceptable; just ask our parents.

And then the world around us weighs in. We read books, watch movies, and hear stories from friends that unconditional love is the secret to building and maintaining a great relationship; that, in order for a relationship to thrive, we need to accept people for who they are. We need to love, understand, and allow them to just be themselves. I would agree, but only in theory, as oftentimes it doesn't turn out that way. Perhaps author Deb Caletti said it best:

"Unconditional love is like a country of two with no laws and no government. Which is all fine and well if everyone is peaceful and

law abiding. In the wrong hands, though, you'll have looting and crime sprees."

Unconditional love works when the dynamics in the relationship remain relatively unchanged over time. Parents love their children unconditionally for a multitude of biological and emotional reasons. And while both parents and children might change as they learn, grow, and mature over time, the relationship oftentimes stays similar to the way it was when it started. It's hierarchical, with the parents holding the dominant position, the children holding the subordinate. The same can be said for pets. Domesticated animals respond to our requests, can be trained to please us, and offer us their loyalty and devotion; all we have to do is feed them. It's a trade, of sorts, and everyone gets what they want and need.

In essence, unconditional love is simply offering love and affection without any limitations. You won't withhold love due to feeling slighted, because you don't feel that way. You won't be offended by their behavior, body language, or tone of voice, because you aren't reading into it. You accept completely. The love you feel and show has relatively no bounds and remains the same regardless of the conditions surrounding the relationship.

It sounds great—perhaps even Utopian—but this kind of love doesn't have a chance in real-world romantic relationships. Behaviors and conversations are subjective and open to interpretation. We are bombarded with responsibility, priorities, challenges, worries, and needs. We want things. Words and actions can be misinterpreted, misconstrued and misunderstood. Perhaps more importantly, our perspectives change. We shift our views about the world, our place in it, the people around us, and ourselves based on what we learn, what our close friends and family have experienced, our workplaces (and the people and shifting dynamics there), and everyday life. And because things shift and change, what we deem as acceptable one minute doesn't work for us the next.

Our Ever-Changing Perspective Defines Our Future

You meet someone and things might instantly click (which is a beautiful thing). However, the relationship isn't going to stay that way. It's not that the relationship isn't going to be great. It's that the two people in the relationship are going to do two things: They are going to reveal inner pieces of themselves over time and they are going to learn new things. So, the person you fall in love with isn't the whole person; it's just a piece of them. As you get to know them, you will learn more about them, but it's a moving target because we are all learning and growing all the time.

And this is where the notion of unconditional love gets tricky. You can offer it from the very beginning, but you can't anticipate all the things you don't know—about them and what they will learn moving forward, or about yourself. There are some things that might not click, and you won't know until you get there. Does that mean you don't love them? No, but you have value, wants and needs, also. As such, you can accept them for who they are, but that doesn't mean they are still a match for you.

When we love someone, we risk a lot. We follow the childhood maxim "Treat others as you want to be treated." So if we want to be loved and accepted unconditionally, we will give our partners unconditional love. However, based on their past, their experiences, and their perspective, they might not be ready to reciprocate that level of love and acceptance. They might back away (feeling too vulnerable), or become angry (feeling trapped or smothered), or they might take advantage of the situation. After all, if you are willing to accept any treatment they can run roughshod over you without any consequences—and there is a big difference between loving someone and being someone's doormat.

A Harsh Truth: We teach people how we want to be loved. Every time we accept and reciprocate good treatment, we show our partners that we value ourselves and that giving us respect and effort is not only required, it's what we deserve. Contrarily, every time we accept bad treatment, we are showing our partners that we do not value ourselves, and that we don't respect ourselves enough to require proper treatment. After all, you can't demand respect when you are actively showing others that you don't respect yourself.

And this is the fundamental reason why unconditional love doesn't work. It's not acceptable for someone to do anything. It's not okay for them to treat you in any way they choose. You have value. You are important. Who you are counts, and they need to recognize it.

DON'T SEEK THEIR ATTENTION. REQUIRE THEIR RESPECT. IT LASTS LONGER AND IS A GENUINE REFLECTION OF HOW THEY FEEL ABOUT YOU.

Does all this mean you're supposed to hold back when entering into a relationship? *Yes... That's precisely what it means.* Taking a risk when starting down the path of love is part of what new relationships are all about. But it needs to be informed risk, meaning they show you a bit of themselves and build your confidence in their intentions. Their actions are a genuine reflection of their true intentions, allowing you to trust them further. Trust and love build over time and are based on experience, safety, non-judgment, and comfort. Headfirst love affairs usually land in one place: in a puddle of heartbreak and tears, wondering how they could treat you so badly.

But what of loyalty? What of loving someone through good times and bad? What about mistakes? I hear you. Mistakes are normal. But people don't make mistakes in a vacuum. Those we love make choices, and those choices can and do have an impact on our lives. And while mistakes are normal—and acceptable—the fallout from those choices might not be.

It's time to value you. YOU matter. YOU are valuable. YOU need to feel it so you can show it to the outside world!

TAKE THE PACT OF SELF-VALUE

Having conditions on love doesn't mean that your love has a price. Nor does creating an atmosphere of "You must treat me right to be with me" mean you are high-maintenance. Both statements translate to you having *high standards*—both for you and for those involved with you. Learning how to set and keep boundaries will maintain your value to you, and will result in others valuing you as well.

EXERCISES

REFLECT. If you don't have conditions or expectations on how someone is allowed to treat you that means they can treat you any way they choose, and you will just deal with it. Without conditions, you have no self-value—and, thus, no value to others. People treat you precisely the way you enable/allow them; if you let them choose your worth then you are only worth something if they say so, and that doesn't work.

Revisit your relationships—romantic, friendships, family, coworkers, and others. Are you showing people that you don't value yourself? Are you not communicating clearly that you matter?

EXPRESS YOUR VALUE. Self-value is shown by how you treat yourself, and how you allow others to treat you. If you don't value you then you will accept what comes. You will find yourself behaving in ways others expect you to behave so that they will like you, yet inwardly you will feel self-critical and judgmental.

It is your right to be who you are, expressing your innermost truths, and not feeling like you must live up to someone else's expectations. You have the right to say, "No," when you mean no, or, "I don't care," when that is what you really feel.

ACTION: Make a two-column list. On the left, write the things you have accepted unconditionally prior to today. These are behaviors or issues you accepted against your better judgment. You might have said yes when you felt no. You might have backed down when you wanted to speak up. On the right, describe what you would do differently if it came up again today. By writing it, you manifest your newfound resolve into remaining a strong individual with limits and boundaries.

FIVE POSITIVE STEPS TO AFFIRM YOUR VALUE

Positive outward efforts results in positive inward feelings. Take action and make change—now.

1. Every night for the next seven days, write down five things that were good about your day. These things

don't have to be major, they might be as simple as a wonderful meal, talking to a friend, or getting through something difficult. Maybe you hit every green light on the way home! Look for the little things, as those are the most important.

2. Visit someone you appreciate. Visit with someone who has made a difference in your life, and talk to them about why you value them.

3. Connect with someone close to you and ask them why they have stayed in your life. Get feedback on what makes you a good friend, and what you have brought to that relationship.

4. If you receive a compliment, accept it with a smile and a simple, "Thank you." They meant it, so own it. When you get home, write it down as a positive thing from your day.

5. Say, "Thank You." Keep your eyes open throughout the day for reasons to say and give thanks. Try to recognize the actions people do every day that might be overlooked—maybe a coworker who always works hard or a friend who always seems willing to listen.

REMINDERS

- You are important. What you want, do and say is valuable.

- You can accept others for who they are, but that doesn't mean they are a match for you and where you are at in your life.

- Be open and honest with yourself and your partner. If you like something, speak up! If you don't, say it straight.

- *Being yourself* also means *being true* to you. Don't pretend your needs aren't important. They are.

THE PACT

· · · · · · · · · ·

BEING RIGHT

"Most people do not listen with the intent to
understand; they listen with the intent to reply."
—*Stephen R. Covey*

Listening is critical in all areas of our lives—from work to relationships to knowing what to pay when we order our morning coffee. But listening is more than just hearing. After all, those born with functional ears are able to hear. At its core, hearing is an automatic response of your brain. Sound comes your way and you hear it; it's effortless. But listening is more than just hearing the sounds and speech directed our way. It's an active process by which we receive what's being offered, evaluate the information, and then formulate a response that conveys our thoughts and feelings about what was said.

It sounds simple, but in romantic relationships sometimes it's anything but easy. We might hear what's said, we might even listen to the meaning behind the words, but we are also paying close attention to tone and inflection and body language. Add to that our past experiences—both in our individual lives as well as our experiences with the person speaking—and one thing becomes clear: We are receiving information based on what we think is being said, and not necessarily the manner in which it is actually being offered. The reason for this is straightforward: The information we receive is subjective, is evaluated by us in real-time, and is based on what we think and believe at the time we receive it.

The reality: What we think we hear isn't necessarily what's being said. How many times have you been sure that you "know" what someone will say (and maybe you were wrong) or heard sarcasm from your partner where there wasn't any or avoided discussing an important issue because you were sure of someone's reaction? These are the tapes that play in our heads, and we allow them to talk us out of healthy interactions and intimacy. They are shadows and reflections of our past traumas, unresolved issues, and feelings of inadequacy. These inner voices smack of our incessant need to avoid judgment, protect us—perhaps unnecessarily—from vulnerability, and prevent us from getting too close to those we struggle to trust.

These are messages from prior experiences that hijack our present. They are triggered by subtle reminders of traumatic situations, issues we thought we left far behind; but here they are, front and center for us to contend with again. It's our old relationships coming into our new ones, which means one thing: As humans, we are the sum of our experiences, but when it comes to hurt, we all tend to live in the past.

And we protect ourselves. We feel the twinge when our partner does something that we remember (even subliminally) as traumatic, and we start in with making sure our partner listens to us. We put our viewpoints out strongly because we feel we are right. And it is here that the real problems start.

COMMUNICATION IS NOT THE CORNERSTONE OF A RELATIONSHIP.

The sources are endless, and they all say the same thing: Communication is what makes relationships work. But for many of us, communication ends up translating as talking. Communication is defined as "the imparting or exchanging of information or news"—the keyword being *exchanging*. And too many people are giving out information, but not receiving it. We might think we're listening, but we aren't. We are just allowing the other person to state their viewpoint so we can quickly retort/retaliate/regurgitate our "correct" viewpoint. We end up advocating our views in our efforts to get the other person to not only understand how we see things, but to ensure that they know that how we see things is right. And if they are doing the same thing, the result is what's called an Advocacy Loop.

Advocacy Loops are easy to fall into, and they happen when the people discussing the issue are intent on being right instead of listening. You put your viewpoint out, they put theirs out, and you either instantly disagree or don't even hear it, because you are again rephrasing or reframing your viewpoint to include a "better" or stronger phraseology. They do the same. Rinse. Repeat.

When we only advocate our viewpoint, we are killing off the very thing that actually makes relationships work well: empathy. Empathy is about understanding someone else's viewpoint. It doesn't mean you automatically agree, nor does it mean that you need to give up your beliefs, thoughts or opinions in favor of theirs. It simply means that you put yourself in their shoes, and that you accept what they are saying as real for *them*. Empathy doesn't have ego or a need to be right; it simply works hard to understand how someone else is experiencing the issue at hand.

Without empathy, we end up in a place where we believe we are not only sure we are right (and we might actually be wrong), we need them to know we are right—and then admit it. We advocate until they see how they are so misguided and say it out loud. In a discussion devoid of empathy, it's not enough that we are right; they need to back down, take accountability and say they are wrong. This is based on a combination of ego, insecurity, control issues, and power games—none of which have a place in a successful relationship. But perhaps more importantly, we should consider this:

In a long-term relationship, there will be many disagreements. Sometimes you will be right, and sometimes they will be right. But who is right doesn't really matter, and it certainly doesn't matter if they admit that they are wrong. What matters is if everyone comes out whole on the other side of the discussion—with their beliefs and dignity intact. What matters is that the couple makes the best decision they can *for themselves and for each other.* In essence, you have a choice: You can be right, or you can be happy, but maybe not both... so pick one.

When we're advocating and not truly listening to our partner, we exhibit a number of behaviors that don't help the situation. These are The Seven Deadly Sins of Advocation.

1. We work to win. Some people view relationships and discussions as win-lose scenarios. They will strive to "win" a discussion, even if that means going in for the kill (meaning: saying the ultimate, off-limits thing that will stop the discussion dead in its tracks, thus "winning" the argument).

2. We get sarcastic. Sarcasm can be a great device for humor or levity, but in a heated discussion, it's a put-down at best. More likely it's criticism, condescension and contempt—none of which will foster a healthy discussion and will also do real long-term damage to the relationship.

3. We blame. It's not our fault; it's *their* fault, right? We want them to take ownership of the problem, and then we are innocent.

4. We get defensive. Being afraid of criticism—or worse, having criticism be a trigger from our past—can create havoc. There's no way to listen if you are busy protecting yourself.

5. We don't trust them. We can't listen if we think they are lying or manipulating us.

6. We want them to be logical or rational. When feelings are raw, sometimes logic and rational thinking go out the window... and they can't necessarily see it happening.

7. We get into problem-solving mode. Men are primally-built as problem solvers, and many women look to solve the issues as well. Sometimes, it's not about solving the situation as much as it is being a sounding board or just discussing the issue.

To stop the process of advocating and instead foster effective communication in your relationships, you need to learn to listen just as much as you need to learn to speak. But it's hard. You might be clear on things from your side, and it's easy to discuss what you feel... It can be much harder to take your thoughts and feelings and put them to the side, and get in touch with how your partner thinks and feels about the same situation—especially if your views don't align.

TAKE THE PACT OF LISTENING

This pact can be summed up in a simple statement: "I will listen more than I speak." Understanding someone's viewpoint and fully listening to their thoughts allows for respect of oneself and those around us.

EXERCISES

Completing the exercises below will allow you to significantly change your listening and communication skills and work toward the following steps to truly healthy discussions.

PRACTICE BEING WRONG. Thinking we are right can be a dangerous thing. It leads us down a path of not seeing other viewpoints, solutions, or possibilities. It can be driven by ego, and it can be hard to let that go. When entering a conversation or argument, instead of pushing your "right" viewpoint, remove your ego and insert humility instead. Start by considering that you might be dead wrong and work the discussion from there.

Reflect on the last heated discussion/argument you were in with your partner. In your journal (or on paper), document the following. This allows you to revisit the situation, look for places where improvement can be made and understand/empathize with their point of view.

- What were my main points?
- What were their main points?

- What did I hear them say? Could they have meant something different?
- Did I listen and empathize, or was I advocating?
- Did I use sarcasm, patronizing statements, blame, or defensiveness to reflect and detract from the conversation?
- Did we reach an agreement?
- How can I improve the process next time?

PRACTICE EMPATHY. You experience things a certain way, and your partner might not see things the same. Continue the exercise above and look at the situation only from their vantage point—even if that means your feelings don't count for a moment. What do they see? How would you see it from their side? What would you want in the situation?

DON'T JUDGE. Allow your partner their views without evaluating every phrase. Remove your power of "deciding" if they are right and just listen. Read an article or editorial about a subject you are passionate about that includes an opposing viewpoint. Read with the intent to understand the opposing view instead of merely reaffirm your position. (Ex: Abortion.)

Key Concept: You don't have to agree with the opposing viewpoint, just practice reading without judging it. Once you can see both sides of the subject you care about from a third person perspective, translating it to your conversations (first person) will come more easily.

DON'T INTERRUPT. Always allow them to finish their views—provided they are putting them out in a respectful manner. When they are done, don't respond right away. Let their words linger a moment and allow yourself to internalize what they've said. Take a breath before responding; count to three in your head. Do something that physically reminds or prohibits you from responding right   away.

KILL OFF BAD BEHAVIORS AND COMMUNICATION PATTERNS. Remove sarcasm, blame, the notion of winning, and defensiveness from your discussions. Work towards empathy and really listening, not merely hearing.

- Don't jump to conclusions about what you see and hear.
- Don't assume you are right and they are wrong.
- Don't assume you are wrong and they are right.
- Don't ask "Why" questions. They tend to make people defensive.

- Don't shut down their words with statements like, "Don't worry about that."
- Don't patronize or preach.

Apply The Five Principles of Effective Listening

1. RECEIVE THE INFORMATION. Don't talk. Instead, just listen to what they are saying. Don't talk over them or finish their sentences. Just listen. Avoid distractions, and don't try to divide your attention between the speaker and something else. Put your cellphone away and turn the TV off. You might want to make an assumption about what the speaker is saying, or what they're about to say. Don't. And don't rehearse your response. Your only job is only to listen. If you start to plan a response, you aren't listening.

2. MAKE SURE YOU UNDERSTAND WHAT WAS SAID. Now that they are finished, make sure you have received the information correctly by asking clarifying questions, or rephrasing certain things you heard to ensure you heard things correctly.

3. REMEMBER AND REFLECT. This might sound similar to Understanding, but it's not quite the same. Remembering what was said allows you to review the

words, information, tone, and body language you just heard and observed. Reflect on the central points of what they said, and begin to look at things the way they see them. You don't necessarily have to agree, but you need to look at it from their viewpoint.

4. EVALUATE. As you begin to formulate a response, remember you are still not a speaker; you are still a listener. You have been looking at things from their point of view, and it is now time to start incorporating your thoughts and feelings into the situation. Your evaluation can include things like separating fact from opinion, reflecting on accusations or blame, understanding hurt feelings vs. reality, and body language, tone, and facial expressions.

5. RESPOND. If you've completed the first four steps, responding should be straightforward. Address the points you heard in an empathic way, removing judgment, blame, or accusations. Speak in statements that discuss how YOU feel, not how THEY did (or didn't do) something. Discuss how you think and feel about what they said and the situation as a whole. Then prepare to listen again.

Listen, reflect, practice empathy, and seek clarification to ensure that your understanding of their views is correct.

The bottom line: If you value them and love them, listen to them.

Key Concepts For Effective Communication

- Stick to one issue. When in a heated discussion, people have a tendency to bring up all the things that are bothering them all at once. It's not possible to address everything. Focus on one topic so your partner can clearly respond to an issue and figure out how to change things.

- Use "I" statements. If you use the word "you" it can put your partner on the defensive. Instead of "You are so disrespectful," consider something like, "I'm upset with how we communicated last week." From there, you can discuss the issue without putting them on guard.

- Avoid using "always" and "never". Life isn't so black and white, and relationships are made up of peaks and valleys. If they are "always" acting some way that really bothers you, you likely wouldn't (or shouldn't) be with them. Keep things in perspective.

THE PACT

. . . .

CONTROL

"No matter how much work you do on yourself or how much effort you put in, you'll never be able to have a relationship with someone who's not ready for you." — Charles J. Orlando

Falling in love is a beautiful thing. Poets pen sonnets about it; composers write symphonies about it. It makes us smile for no specific reason and fills our hearts with happiness. But falling in love is a very scary thing. It involves acknowledging that we want something we don't have; that we need something that makes us happy. It's pure vulnerability. When we put our feelings out for our partner to evaluate (and hopefully address), we are exposing ourselves to a combination of things we fear. We worry that we will be rejected. We are concerned they will think we are stupid (or needy, or high-maintenance) for what we want. We risk being ridiculed. And—perhaps our biggest worry—we are afraid to lose them.

These feelings can lead to shifts in our behavior… shifts that emanate from one place: fear. If we've experienced challenging situations in our past—bad relationships or break-ups, family issues or divorce, feelings of abandonment or being bullied or shunned—it can magnify our feelings of vulnerability, and intensify our need to stay safe. In essence, we feel insecure. And when people are insecure, they seek security; they seek control.

And we silently (or subconsciously) convince ourselves that our safety is dependent on our ability to control things. Which means: We feel the need to protect ourselves from getting hurt emotionally, so we take steps to ensure we have control of things. But it is here that things run amuck. Most people don't like being controlled, told what to do, or made/forced to do things they wouldn't normally do. As such, a fissure in the relationship is instantly created—although perhaps not immediately seen by either party—becoming more apparent and widening as the need for control and/or controlling behavior continues.

People who vie for control are usually doing so as a reaction to fear. That fear can be based on not wanting to be at the mercy of others, from traumatic events or past relationships that left them vulnerable, hurt or devastated, or a deep-rooted insecurity that they haven't solved. Due to these issues, they might feel they *need* control of any and all things in their domain, and it manifests itself in unhealthy ways.

This need for control oftentimes surfaces in their friendships and romantic relationships. These controlling people might feel an incessant need to micromanage people and activities, orchestrate the actions and behaviors of others, or maintain rigid routines and rules—not only for themselves, but for others as well.

Are you with a control freak?

In any relationship, it's normal for power and control to pass back and forth between both people. It can shift during times of need (example: child-rearing), when one person specializes in a certain issue (example: finances or home furnishings), or other situations. If, by looking at your relationship, you can't see a "boss" between the two of you, it's likely that neither of you have control issues. As such, you both likely pass the Baton of Power between you very well, and your relationship is equal.

However, many relationships exist that are one-sided, and the behavior manifests itself in myriad ways. A controlling person:

- Usually needs to be in-charge of things and activities.

- Might think they are only "overprotective", but in reality they are jealous to the point of ridiculousness, and they might keep tabs on their partner's daily activities, friends, driving patterns, behaviors, clothing choices and more.

- The breadwinner of the relationship might keep a tight rein on money and finances without visibility to their partner.

- Could constantly tell their partner the "right way" to do things, and never listen to others' opinions or suggestions.

- If they have children, they feel they know "what's right" to the point of pushing their partner into the background.

Relationships don't *usually* begin with one or both people acting like control freaks—and if they do, that red flag is glaring and apparent. Dating and the get-to-know-you process are fun and full of mystery and intrigue. Most times, if someone shows controlling behavior, the other person will recognize things and get clear before the relationship goes too far. The problems usually occur after some time has passed—needs start being met, sexual boundaries have been crossed, and a relationship has been forged. Control issues then manifest themselves as statements and behaviors that are clearly not good, but the controlling person frames them up as positive—or worse, as not their fault.

The controlling person will go to great lengths to get their own way; they can be disrespectful, manipulative, intimidating, highly critical, and will twist the truth while debating issues and having discussions.

Eight Ways Controlling People Assert Themselves

1. BLAME. They shift the argument to seem as though it's always their partner's fault. No matter how the discussion goes or the reality of the situation, it's something their partner did that either triggered or caused the problem.

2. DISCOUNTING. A controlling person will make it clear that their partner's feelings and/or needs are wrong, misguided, or somehow invalid.

3. ABANDONMENT. By action or word, a controlling person will make it clear that they will leave if their partner doesn't agree or back down.

4. GUILT. Shame is a weapon in these cases, and the person being controlled will feel badly for not agreeing or doing what the other person wants— oftentimes thinking something like, *It will be easier if I just agree and/or let things go.*

5. SHIFTING. A controlling person will shift and/or derail a conversation to gain advantage and move the focus to a subject they can maneuver through, usually after falsely acknowledging how the other person feels and then moving on without really addressing the issue at hand.

6. WITHDRAWING LOVE AND SUPPORT. The most common behavior from controlling people is to withdraw pleasure or supportive actions from the other person. In effect, the controlled person is "punished" and the controlling person spends time away from their partner to "teach them a lesson".

7. THREATS AND INTIMIDATION. A controlling person might threaten to do something—find another lover, take children away, enter imposingly into personal space—as a means of control.

8. VIOLENCE. Any person who resorts to physical violence isn't just a controlling person; *they are an abuser.* Get help from a trusted friend, spiritual advisor, co-worker, or family member immediately.

And it can start *very* slowly... so slowly, in fact, that these damaging behaviors might show themselves in seemingly innocuous ways:

*   Controlling statements or questions said under the guise of, "I just care about you, so I want to know."

*   Phone calls and texts at any/all hours. If the receiver feels checked on or controlled, they are told something akin to, "I was just worried about you," or "I just wanted to make sure you were okay."

*   Negative statements framed up as "protective" or "caring" about friends or family, usually laying the groundwork for larger control issues later.

- Comments/verbal jabs about weight, food/meal choices, clothing, job, or hobbies that they feel are "in your best interest" or they insist that they are telling you because they "just love you."

And because of how "caring" these comments and behaviors might first appear, it can be very easy to get tangled up and think you are just misreading things; that *you* must be the problem. Besides, they love you and it's only right to receive their comments and value their opinion, right? But here's the rub: It's great to value what they think and say, but not at the expense of your own thoughts and opinions about you, your value, or what you believe you should do/be doing. By putting their opinions and statements above your own, you are slowly putting yourself under their thumb—and within their control.

It's a pattern that repeats. Before you know it you will be thinking that you are *always* doing something wrong. You will start second-guessing yourself and your decisions. You won't be able to figure out if it's them (you think it might be when you're away from them), or if it's you (like they always tell you). You'll start to feel anxious around them, and you'll think you can make things right again if you just [insert newest idea that might please them here]. You'll do whatever you must to get back to the way you both felt at the beginning of the relationship. But the thing that will keep you up at night is the haunting thought that their opinions of you are right, that there are things wrong with you (their list grows weekly), and you are not lovable or worthy of love the way you are.

If these statements and situations are ringing bells, you are in a controlling relationship and you need to make some serious changes. Note that by shifting the balance of power, things will often get worse before they get better and the relationship may show itself as unchangeable, meaning you are better off leaving than continuing to try to fix a situation that is unsalvageable. After all, you can only change *you*; you can't change or fix *them*.

Five Steps To Control Recovery

1. Find a time that's calm and get honest. To make change, both of you need to be in an accepting place. Share your concerns and your feelings. If they get aggressive, *hold your ground.* Acquiescing to their needs, thoughts or opinions is what this issue is about! You can listen and be supporting of their views, but not at the expense of your own. (*Note: If*

you can't get past this step, you are likely in a situation that isn't workable for recovery.)

2. Speak slowly and agree not to engage—both of you. When a controlling person is doing their thing, they often increase both the speed and volume of their speech, and they might take an intimidating physical stance. If you stand your ground, you will both end up in an all-out fight. To counter this, slow the conversation down and *think* before you speak by counting to five *before you respond.*

3. Set clear limits. Let your partner know that you are open to hearing their thoughts and feelings, but you will no longer engage in conversations that attack who you are as a person or your behavior. Repeat this and get acknowledgement that they understand the rules.

4. Make your demands. Be clear with what the issues are and how they are affecting you. Ask them if they are trying to hurt you. Explain what their behavior is doing to you emotionally and how it is driving you away.

5. Take a timeout, if needed. Stopping the conversation is a useful way to prevent arguments from escalating.

If things become heated or the conversation starts to move into areas that are not beneficial to solving the problems, call a timeout. Note that a timeout is not a weapon that can be used as a measure of control. It is used to quell anxiety or anger, not as a tool to cause further damage. The maximum time limit for a timeout is 60 minutes—and ideally someone will leave the physical location for that duration to allow both parties to cool off.

It's important to note that these techniques will not work unless both parties are willing to invest in positive change—both for the relationship and each other. It's possible that things won't improve, despite your best efforts. In some cases, a controlling partner may get worse. If things improve, great! But if not, your best option is probably to get out while your self-esteem is still intact.

Relationships should support your growth, not bring you down and make you doubt your own worth. Love celebrates you; it doesn't try to show you how you are unacceptable for the person you are. You deserve to have a great, loving relationship. So start with yourself, and love yourself enough to take the first step in reclaiming you, if that's what needs to happen.

If YOU are the one who is controlling

Sometimes we just want to help. But when things shift into ugly places—like those outlined above—it creates conflict, resentment, anger, and a loss of intimacy and connection—even if it's not evident immediately. Even if your intentions are good (as far as you're concerned) it doesn't matter. What *does* matter is how those intentions are received. If we try to show our love by offering unsolicited advice and opinions, or by making unreasonable demands, it only pushes friends and loved ones away.

If you are in a place where you are being told you are controlling your loved ones, it's time to make some changes.

Four Steps To Stop Controlling Behavior

1. Know this: You aren't perfect. None of us are. We are learning and growing. Perhaps you have some good ideas and opinions, but just because you have them doesn't make you *right*. Your opinions are right *for you*.

2. Focus on the positive. We all have things that need improvement, but by complaining and telling people about their faults, it communicates two things: 1) That

you are dissatisfied with who they are as a person; and 2) That you know what's best for them and they don't. Instead of complaining about or trying to change someone to fit your version of who they "should be", focus on their positive qualities. Think about what you like and appreciate about them. And then think about ways you can improve yourself for the better.

3. Listen attentively without solving anything. Sometimes people want assistance in solving issues. But many times they are just looking for a sounding board to bounce things off so they can solve their own issues. If you love them, you don't have to solve it all. You can just be there to listen. Open ears and a closed mouth go far in showing support… and they'll ask if they need your thoughts on how to solve things.

4. Adjust your expectations. Expecting too much from people fuels controlling actions that lead to disappointment and resentment on both sides. It's great to have high standards, so long as they aren't unreasonable and don't require someone to completely shift who they are to fit some unrealistic expectation you have of them. A reality check: Your partner isn't going to address *all* your needs; that's not their job.

TAKE THE PACT OF RELEASE

The time has come for you stop being controlled and to relinquish your attempts to control those around you. The reality is: You can't control anyone or make them change; they choose their own path and make their own decisions. You can support them, love them and be a partner/lover/friend, but, ultimately, their path is theirs. They can *share* that path with you, but it is *their path*.

EXERCISES

REFRAME YOUR DEFINITION OF LOVE. Too often, we get "love" mixed up with control (or being controlled). It's important to know a real definition of love. Please read the below every day as you evaluate control in your relationships.

Love is not sacrifice; it is understanding. Love is not compromise of one's core desires; it is reciprocal encouragement of what both want and need. Love is not fear of loss; it is acknowledgement that control of someone else is not yours. Love is not telling half-truths; it is honor, trust, and respect, for them and for yourself. Ultimately, love is about vulnerability, allowing someone to see that you want them in your life, and trusting them enough not to hurt you.

REVISIT YOUR PAST AND GET PERSPECTIVE. If you are experiencing (or have experienced) some or all of the control issues outlined in this chapter (as a controlling person or as the unwilling/unwitting recipient of controlling behavior), grab a piece of paper and make a list ... and prepare to get honest. On the left, list your behaviors. Are you being manipulative (or being manipulated)? Do you give (or receive) guilt as a weapon (as a means of control)? By calling it out, you grant yourself awareness and now you can effect change.

On the right side, list the reasons you are causing (or allowing) the behavior. Are you afraid based on something in your past? Do you feel inadequate? Are you unhappy with yourself? With your partner? With the relationship? Are you lashing out as a means of feeling better because of [insert reason here]. Now share the list with your partner and give them visibility into how you feel. Ideally, your partner will make a list at the same time (separately from you), and you can share with each other. If you are single, share it with a trusted friend and ask them if it's a fair assessment of your behavior in previous relationships. With that insight, you can focus on changing those behaviors to avoid them in the future.

PRACTICE THE SERENITY MEDITATION. In our lives, there are things we can control and things we simply cannot. It is important to know the difference to avoid frustration, stress, and possible heartache. To that end, I offer the Serenity Meditation (also known as the Serenity Prayer):

> *May I have the Serenity to accept the things I cannot change, the Courage to change the things I can, and the Wisdom to know the difference.*

Read this meditation daily. Write it down, and keep it in a place where you can see or access it easily. While reflecting on this meditation/prayer for the first time, consider the following:

- Reflection on things you cannot change. Get a sheet of paper. On one side, list things you can control (your time, when you put gas in your car, how loud the ringer is on your phone, your reactions, the way you allow others to treat you). On the other side, list things you cannot (the weather, the line for coffee, the longest red light in the world, other people's reactions and behavior). Note: It might sound silly when you start, but nothing is too small. The smaller the issues you focus on the more you can truly notice what is and is not within your control.

- Reflection on Courage. Make a list of everything that gives you courage—friends, a higher power/God, a song, a favorite poem, anything that makes you feel strong and courageous. Then revisit the list you made of things you can control. What is one step you can take (using your courage list) to effect change on the list of things you can change? How would you continue to do this moving forward?

- Reflection on Serenity. Using the same two-step process, list everything that gives you peace or comfort—a cup of tea, soft music, praying, yoga/meditation, a good friend, breathing). Then revisit the list of items you cannot control. What mechanisms for finding peace can you use to find serenity and accept the things you cannot control? Give yourself permission to relinquish control of these things and be okay with it.

Above all, realize that you can't control anyone. You can't make them do anything or be something they don't want to be. Ultimately, everyone is precisely who they are, and the only control you have is if you accept them and if they are a fit for you. If they aren't, stop trying to mold them (or yourself) into something they are (or you're) not. Life is too short.

THE PACT

LOVE BLOCK #9

· · · · · · · · · · ·

COMPLACENCY

"The tragedy of life is often not in our failure, but rather in our complacency; not in our doing too much, but rather in our doing too little; not in our living above our ability, but rather in our living below our capacities." — *Benjamin E. Mays*

Dating starts much like an interview for that dream job you always wanted. You plan things out, wear your best clothes, and primp and prepare. You're excited about the opportunity and the possibilities, and you are completely involved. Then: You get the job, and you're all-in. It's the Honeymoon Period—the job loves you, you love the job, and everything is perfect. Fast-forward 6-12 months at that same dream job, and you'll find many people who have dropped back in their passion, dedication, and effort. They don't put in the same amount of effort. They aren't as passionate about what they are doing. Things have become a bit more predictable, and the excitement has waned a bit. And at the extreme, some people are just going through the motions—uninterested and simply staying because it's familiar. Sadly, many relationships follow this same protocol.

When relationships start, everyone puts in as much effort as possible. It's a time of happiness, positivity, optimism, and energy. Then … things can slow down. The humdrum of life and cohabitation get in the way. At the beginning, you couldn't wait to see them; now the dread of the commute home cancels out whatever/whomever might be waiting for you. Dates were initially all about creating the mood of romance, seduction, and happiness, but sharing time has been replaced by brief, weekly dinner dates of two or three hours. The days of discovery and fun discussion are limited (if they happen at all), and are largely replaced by "talks" centered on what makes the household function: kids, finances, chores, and schedules. Sex shifts from hot passion and desire—with massages and showers together—to the same-old-same-old 11½ minutes of predictable foreplay and intercourse—the conclusion (as opposed to climax) of which merits a fast cleanup with a washcloth in the sink, and a silent rollover to get some sleep.

WITHOUT A SIGNIFICANT CHANGE AND A
SERIOUS WAKE-UP CALL, RELATIONSHIPS
THAT ARE BORING, COMPLACENT, AND
WITHOUT SPONTANEITY WILL END.

But this isn't the way it's supposed to be, is it?
We're taught from childhood that you look for your soul
mate or somehow your soul mate finds you—"Someday
my prince (or princess) will come." It's the Disney Effect;
we are living our lives calmly, and then from nowhere—
BAM! We're in love, and it's perfect and amazing. Sure, it
can happen. But more often than not, lasting love is built
with effort, passion, and appreciation, it doesn't just
appear. Too often, "love at first sight" transforms into
expecting them to be there. And it can lead to a feeling of
being taken for granted.

DON'T TAKE THEM FOR GRANTED.
NO MATTER HOW MUCH SOMEONE
LOVES YOU, EVERYONE HAS THEIR
LIMIT FOR FEELING UNAPPRECIATED.

What people do for each other is supposed to
matter—as trite as that might sound—and not just at the

start, but also throughout the relationship. From the time we are toddlers, we are taught to treat others as we wish to be treated. What we actually *do* for each other might not be identical—as we all have different things that we interpret as giving and/or receiving love (vis-à-vis *The 5 Love Languages* by Gary D. Chapman)—but we want our efforts to be appreciated. Whether it's as complicated as helping them rebuild a car motor or simply doing the dishes or writing a love note, we want our efforts to be noticed and appreciated by those we love. And no one is perfect. We slip and might accidentally miss something, and that's just human. But when efforts and support aren't acknowledged over a period of time, we may feel unappreciated. Feeling unappreciated provides a perfectly (read: awful) combination of resentment, contempt, and hurt that will sound the death knell for any relationship. Without any measure of joint learning, growth, or appreciation, the relationship has entered The Doldrums.

The Doldrums are a period of time that reflects inactivity, stagnation, or depression. All relationships and marriages have peaks and valleys, things happen internally within the marriage and externally that affect the relationship—good and bad. But when feelings of discontent last for an extended period of time—with no sign of change forthcoming—that's not a valley or rough spot in the relationship; it's a way of life.

The state of a relationship is most-often reflected in the little things—the small behaviors that we might not notice until they are gone. When kisses goodbye or good night slowly stop, handholding disappears, and midday calls cease, you have the beginnings of a break-up. Those little things are actually unspoken intimacies that are required for connection in a long-term relationship; a continuation of dating long after they are a "sure-thing."

You can be sure you're in The Doldrums when:

- Your communication is limited to family issues, finances, or essential information
- Most of your relationship has transferred to either the phone or text messages
- Your sex life has dwindled to once a week... perhaps less. Even then it's very predictable and focused on the physical
- You aren't having any fun

Left unchecked, things may escalate:

- Your communication is reduced to only critical issues, and you're okay with it
- Casual, impromptu affection is not only nonexistent, but you don't think of it
- You pick fights so you can steer clear of them

- You're happier alone than with your partner
- You feel like an option in your partner's life
- You think about breaking up or start to imagine what your life will/would be like on your own

The Doldrums can be fought through, if the situation is identified and discussed openly and honestly. However, it's very easy to move from these escalated issues to something worse: indifference.

Being comfortable is one thing, but once you stop caring what they do or don't do, your relationship is already over. Indifference is even worse than complacency, because it's not satisfaction or contentment, it's a pure take-it-or-leave-it attitude that will come through in everything you do, say, or communicate. And if you have no feelings either way, then it's done.

COMPLACENCY AND INDIFFERENCE
ARE THE CATALYSTS FOR DISCONNECTION
AND SEPARATION. THE CURE: PASSION FOR
EACH OTHER, AND LUST FOR LIFE.

Marriage and love mean different things to different people, but there is a very common societal viewpoint on both: The overarching goal is to connect and to share about everything: all your wants, needs, hopes, failures, wishes, experiences, and desires. We enter into a relationship with a certain set of expectations, but those expectations can and will change over time. And why? Because we are all learning, experiencing, and growing. As we experience new things and our life plan shifts, it's natural to have our expectations of others shift as well. But what can kill things—or send people into places of separation and disconnection—is not communicating the changes *as they change*. By not including them in things that shift for you, you are implying that they aren't important in your future. In essence, you are silently (and perhaps unintentionally) advising them that they don't need to know certain things—because they might not be with you as your life moves forward. Communicate what changes for you. Keep them in the loop with what matters, because *they* matter.

Personal Complacency

Many times, there can be a fundamental disconnection right from the start of a relationship, and it can be traced back to an old maxim: Men fall in love with a woman thinking she *won't* change, but she does; women fall in love with a man thinking that he *will* change, but he doesn't. In truth, *everything* is always changing, always in motion. As humans, we are always learning, growing, striving… And if that stops for us as individuals, that static, stoic way of being will push back into the relationship. In truth, the moment we stop learning and growing, we get comfortable. When we feel *satisfied*, then we start to relax. But is feeling of satisfaction "wrong"?

In *The Hazy Moon of Enlightenment* (Wisdom Publications, 2007), the late Taizan Maezumi Roshi wrote, "Our life is always fulfilled in just the right way. We have this life, we live it, and this is enough. In the best sense, having few desires is to realize this. Yet, somehow, we think something is lacking, and so we have all kinds of desires." This viewpoint is central to the Four Noble Truths, which comprise the essence of Buddha's teachings. In Buddhism, the cause of suffering (called "dukkha") is craving or desire. The notion is that, because we see ourselves as small and limited, we go through life trying to grab one thing after another to make us feel bigger or safer. Freeing ourselves from this desire leads to *satisfaction*.

While I would never be so bold as to argue or disagree with the teachings of Buddha, I would strongly suggest that much of mankind is not prepared to sit idle and allow existence to wash over them in a "satisfied" state of mind. In today's world, we are all on a quest. Some seek fortune, others fame, and still others look for connection and enlightenment. That quest is likely life-long for most of us (sans His Holiness, The Dalai Lama). As such, it matters not what direction you grow and learn; the important thing is to *keep growing and keep learning*. To stop is to languish in feelings of discontent and mediocrity, and in reflection of today's society, it will stop you from achieving the life you want—and, in connection, the love life you want as well. Perhaps there will come a time when a truly peaceful, connected society exists where people are without desire and want for nothing. When that time comes, I will happily rewrite this section and have an updated edition published. Until then, I offer this: Keep learning and putting effort into what makes you tick.

Being completely satisfied is not necessarily part of the human condition. From the beginning of human history, we—as a species—have continually progressed and grown. We evolved from hunters/gatherers in caves to the beginnings of agriculture and small communities all the way to the Industrial (and now Technological) Revolution. We, as humans, strive for more: knowledge, love, happiness, faith, passion... it's endless. A recognition that wants and needs will change over time allows for people to move past a feeling of acceptance and complacency.

And when it comes to growth, we all, actually, have no choice. We can choose the direction in which we grow—for better, for worse—but we *will grow* regardless of our efforts to stop. The key is to share what we are learning back into our relationships. It keeps us connected, and allows the relationships to flourish. After all, relationships are made up of individuals, and those individuals will direct that relationship's success—or failure.

TAKE THE PACT OF CONTINUED GROWTH

To keep things fresh and engaged in life and love, it's necessary to continue your learning and growth, growing beyond the sum of your own parts, so to speak. Learning new things and then sharing them back into the relationship keeps things new, fresh and strong—not only for the couple, but also for the individuals.

Exercises For The Disconnected Relationship

RECONNECT. If life has taken its toll and you have just realized that things are disconnected, it can be a very shocking realization. Now that you know, it's important to take action. If you are resentful or upset that your partner hasn't taken action before this time, please remember that life is not perfect—and you have also just realized what's going on.

To get back on track, you need to reconnect:

STEP ONE: ESTABLISH VALUE. When talking about something difficult or vulnerable, it's critical to reach out and explain why they matter. Be open and tell them how you are feeling. Explain that they—and the relationship—are important to you, which is why you are talking. Use statements that show them they matter.

- "I care about you and our relationship."
- "It's been a rough road for some time now, but I want you to know that I'm right here and I'm not going anywhere."
- "You are important, and I love you."

STEP TWO: STATE YOUR NEEDS. Discussing how you value them as a person and how they fit in your life is the starting point, and reflects how you feel *today*. Your wants and needs are about what needs to be addressed *in the future*. This is best done by not blaming or accusing for what hasn't happened or who hasn't done what; that discussion will be nonproductive and likely lead you down a path of further disconnection. Talk about what you want—more time together, a date night, more fun ... whatever your needs are. And while you can't predict or control how they will react to your needs, you can put it out there openly and honestly.

STEP THREE: MAKE A PLAN. Once you have your needs put out plainly, you can discuss theirs as well. And from there, you can *both* form the plan that allows you to fill your needs and reconnect. If you are missing time together, get your calendars out and make a date! If life has become all about the kids and their activities, shift things around and make your relationship a priority! If work and finances are in the way, consider shifting things around and reprioritizing things—before it's too late.

1. WHAT DO YOU LOVE ABOUT THEM? Sometimes, when things get disconnected or things become routine, we have a hard time remembering the good things, the fun, or the things that we have in common. Each of you should make list of 10-20 traits, activities, or behaviors that you love about the other. Do this separately. When finished, come back together and take turns reading one item at a time to each other. Discuss why you put each item on the list.

2. SAY HELLO MIDWAY THROUGH THE DAY. Set some time to connect part way through the day. It doesn't have to be a long conversation, just a few minutes to touch base (via voice, *not a text message*) and see how their day is shaping up.

3. IT'S THE LITTLE THINGS. Rekindle the little affections. Hold hands as you walk, sit on the same couch when watching TV, and tell them you love them.

4. END THE DAY TOGETHER. So often, it's bedtime when couples really disconnect. Go to bed together and fall asleep with each other. Do this for two straight weeks before shifting schedules. And then, if schedules shift, don't allow more than two days to pass without retiring for the evening together.

ADVANCED WORK

TAKE A CLASS. Research a dance or cooking class in your area. Take it together, as a team. It's not only a new experience, but it will also require that you connect and work together.

SCHEDULE A TECH-FREE DAY. Pick a day each week where you both (and kids, if you have them) put all technology away. Spend real-world time with real people. Once you set the day, *don't move it no matter what.*

DO SOMETHING SPONTANEOUS. Seriously! Love is supposed to be fun, remember? Like it was at the beginning. You might be a few years away from where you started, but get back to what pulled you two together. Talk about your favorite date … and relive it.

NOT IN A RELATIONSHIP YET?

DO THE WORK. Preparing for love can mean changing things—perhaps even a drastic shift from how things were done in your past relationships. To be prepared for a lasting relationship that is connected, please revisit the first eight chapters of this book. From there, you can apply what you've learned to your new partner, once they enter the picture.

PREPARE. Do some introspection. Make a list and identify ways in which you experienced or displayed complacency or indifference in past relationships. Knowing where you've come from is a way to avoid the same pitfalls in your journey ahead.

DON'T RUSH IN. Once you meet someone of interest, allow things to evolve over time. It will lead to discovery, and keep things fresh for both of you.

THE PACT

. . . .

IGNORING YOUR PASSION

"I can teach anybody how to get what they want out of life. The problem is that I can't find anybody who can tell me what they want." –Mark Twain

When we're kids, we have crazy, incredible dreams and aspirations. Our goals are lofty and amazing. We want to be astronauts and parents and archeologists and doctors and artists and actors and fashionistas and architects and veterinarians and racecar drivers and hair stylists and presidents of countries and nurses and dog walkers. We want to help and build and extend and grow and reach for the stars. We dream big because there are no limits to our thoughts and aspirations. We practice by dressing up and playing pretend, and we shift our dreams at a moment's notice—a cowboy one second, and a gourmet chef the next.

Then we are introduced to what others call "reality". *They* and we assess our skills and choices are presented. The standard question: "What do you want to be when you grow up?" The message is clear: You have to *choose* now—and it sounds and feels finite. We are no longer unbounded; those who would decide if our life's passion is worthy now limit us. We continue to narrow our options based on a combination of things we hear and others' expectations of what we should do:

- "You can't do that."
- "That won't pay the bills."
- "Do you *really* want to be [insert profession here]?"
- "We worked hard so that you can go to college."
- "Why would you [insert choice here]? That's just not smart."

These and countless other statements fuel our own doubt, and it is compounded by our self-imposed limits. We decide that we can't do [whatever] because of [whatever], and, before long, life has taken over. 17 years old becomes 25, then 40, and the dreams we had are washed over by day-to-day life—careers, bills, kids, marriage, commutes, laundry and expectations ad nauseam. It's the noise and expectations of life. Our passions have been replaced by the notion of what's needed and required by others, not by our own wants and desires for ourselves. In effect, our dreams have been narrowed down.

Part of that is normal. Living in today's society requires that a living be made. Money needs to be generated to pay bills, and the needs of others who count on us must—and should—be addressed. And there are limits for what we are able to accomplish, based on a variety of criteria. To wit: If your lifelong dream is to be a jet fighter pilot, and your eyesight isn't 20/20, you're not able to make that happen. That limit is about ability and practicality—even safety. It's not based on limits that are based on expectations others have, or rules that have been self-imposed due to doubt, fear, or denial of what you truly want.

The real issue arises when we ignore our passions and live a life based solely on responsibility. When we concentrate on our obligation and don't address our passions, then we are merely *existing, not living*—and certainly not living a life based on our True Self. This doesn't mean everyone should drop what they are doing, throw practicality to the wind, ignore bills and finances and start painting as their family wallows in destitution. What it *does* mean is that ignored passions and dreams have a way of nagging at you. They come out as resentment, contempt, and anger, usually at yourself, but it can also be directed to those around you in an effort to "blame" them for what is missing inside you.

IF WE PURSUE GOALS THAT DO NOT REFLECT WHO WE REALLY ARE AND WHAT WE CARE ABOUT, THEN EVEN IF WE ACHIEVE THOSE GOALS, WE ARE NOT GOING TO FEEL HAPPY OR FULFILLED.

When we aren't living true to our passions, we are filled with excuses and reality checks that justify why we aren't doing what we *want* … we are only doing what we *should* or *need* to do. When we make a choice or we say something that is not in alignment with our True Self, things happen. Some people get an ugly pang in their gut. Others might wake up with a feeling of sadness or disconnection. These feelings are the physical manifestations of guilt, the guilt for not being true to your soul. They can be ignored or stifled it, but they won't stay buried long. In truth, these feelings are a virtual tap on the shoulder by the universe that we aren't being true to *ourselves*.

The most common behaviors of someone not living in alignment with their True Self is that they procrastinate and/or make excuses for not doing what really matters to them, or they fill themselves with negative self-talk. They justify why they aren't acting on their passions with "meaningful" reasons for what they *should be doing* or what they *need to do*. Other times, these same people might live a life of distraction, creating and/or bringing chaos into their lives as a means to avoid what they want most. But perhaps the most damaging thought is one that so many conjure: "It's too late to do what I want to do." That nefarious thought hits with myriad punches: too fat, too thin, too out, too in, too busy, too broke, too much trouble, too many assholes, too much baggage, too little time, too much drama, too many bills, too late, too old... STOP!

YOU AREN'T TOO LATE.
YOU ARE RIGHT ON TIME.

We are all on our path, and we get to things when we do. It's not a matter of "being late". *What's important is that you have arrived at this point on your journey.* Age, issues, time passing, kids, marriages, jobs… all those things are important, but they cannot and will not hinder you from chasing down your passion unless you give it that power.

Example From Society:

In the 1980s, there was a man featured as a guest on The Tonight Show with Johnny Carson. He was a real estate agent; one of the best there was at the time. He was a master of flipping property— buying houses and buildings low, fixing them up, and selling them for a profit. What made him different was that he started his career at an unusual age—74 years old. On the show, he revealed that he was presently 103 years old and that he had just taken out a 30-year mortgage on a property he was planning on keeping—approved for the loan because his credit was impeccable. He shared that his past careers included bartending, engineering, and horticulture, but he always wanted to develop property and land. He loved creating and improving something and then allowing someone else to enjoy it. His demeanor was impassioned, but calm and centered. He had embraced his passions and his True Self.

This man's story is an important reflection, as he wasn't stifled by societal demands or self-imposed limitations. He had already done many things, and therein lies the main point. Your True Self is defined by how you feel at that time in your life and in accordance with your experience and your changing/shifting interests and passions. As kids, we are maneuvered down a path of "you need to *pick* something to do with your life." But in truth, you have the option to change your mind, choose something new, and/or discover things about yourself. You can choose.

We are all many things: moms or dads, sons or daughters, providers, drivers, but that doesn't define us. We can be more than one thing. Our True Selves aren't limited in capacity, only by our own doubts and distractions.

Many times, however, we get things out of order. We try to take people on a journey when we don't know where we are actually headed. Or we try to decide our life partner without considering how they connect with our True Self. This is a set-up for failure, in that we need to have a sense of what we want from our life *before* we invite someone to go on that journey with us. Without a discovery of our True Self, we don't really have a sense of compatibility with others. Can we discover part of that *with* our partners? Yes, but True *Self* is about us, not them. It's much easier to focus externally (as distraction) rather than get introspective on what we actually want from life. It's actually much easier to walk through life *not* knowing who we are or what our True Self passion is; ignorance is bliss. The hard work is in uncovering where our passions lie, and then acting on them.

Uncovering your True Self can lead to a great deal of confusion. Often people want to control things. They want to plan out where they are going and how they will get there. The problem is that doesn't work. You can do *your* work, but you also have to leave some things up to the universe—meaning: you doing your part and walking your path of self-discovery is 50 percent of things. 25 percent is then up to the universe to potentially align with your wants and needs; the remaining 25 percent is chance. Chance plays a big part in things, and it is one of the reasons why all journeys are exciting. You can't control it all. In matters of life and love, you can choose your destination, or you can choose how you will get there, but most times you can't plan and control both. Sometimes the unexpected dictates the outcome, and the only way to get what you want is to surrender.

Personal Thoughts:

We are taught at a very young age that if we want something, we should go and get it! Be tenacious! Be audacious! Be strong and chase it down! These statements and more have been my mantras for most of my life. However, there is more. (And isn't there always?) The reality is: You can only have that go-getter attitude on YOUR side of the equation. Life and other people still have to do their part(s). Sometimes, you can do your part, and then... you don't push-and-push-and-push-and-PUSH. Instead, you surrender. You allow Life to do its job—to shift and adjust according to not only what you want/need/hope for but also to make space for what IT has planned. You can call it God, Mohammad, Faith, the Universe... whatever. Free will, choice, and tenacity can bring you most of the way to your goals, but sometimes you have to surrender so that you can succeed.

As you head down a path of self-evaluation and discovery, you will find something out very quickly: Not everything will work out as you think or plan. Failure and/or setbacks are not only normal; they are critical to our growth. It doesn't matter how many things you try or how many times you attempt and fail. What matters is how you persevere and how you continue to fulfill the wants and dreams of your True Self.

FAILURE IS NORMAL.
YOU WIN SOME; YOU LEARN SOME.

TAKE THE PACT OF TRUE SELF

Combining all these newfound skills leads to a commitment to be true to one's soul. Ultimately, everyone is in charge of their own happiness, but it takes a conscious effort to stay on the path. Setbacks, mistakes and delays are normal… and that's why life is a journey, not a destination.

To keep things fresh and engaged in life and love, it's necessary to continue your learning and growth, growing beyond the sum of your own parts, so to speak. Learning new things and then sharing them back into the relationship keeps things new, fresh and strong—not only for the couple, but also for the individuals.

EXERCISES

GET SPECIFIC ABOUT THE PERSON YOU ARE. We are all on a journey of discovery. We find things and activities that matter to us, uncover pieces of ourselves that we didn't know existed. We reveal strengths that surprise us. To get to the core of who you are, you need to ask yourself important questions about what matters to you. Keep in mind that the answers to these questions will change over time—as you learn new things, gain experience, and live through key life events.

These are living questions that you should ask yourself every six to nine months. They will not only guide you to your True Self, they will create thinking that is critical to ensure your life is filled with meaning—for you and those around you.

SIX QUESTIONS FOR TRUE SELF-DISCOVERY

Get introspective. Get honest. Get real with yourself.

1. WHAT DRIVES ME? This isn't a question about your favorite color or your dream vacation. What *moves* you? What *inspires* you? These passions are part of who you are and what make you tick *in your soul.*

2. WHERE AM I RIGHT NOW IN MY LIFE? Do you identify with what you are doing, or are you simply going through the motions of what's needed? Are you happy? Are you inspired? Do you feel that what you're doing reflects who you are as a person? Are you living in your comfort zone out of fear or obligation? Does that align with your passions and drivers?

3. WHAT WOULD MY PURPOSE BE IF I KNEW NO ONE WOULD JUDGE ME? If cash, responsibilities, and obligations didn't matter and you had a blank slate to work with, what would your life

purpose be? What would you want to do—for you and for others? How does that fit with your current efforts and path?

4. AM I SURROUNDED BY PEOPLE WHO LOVE AND ENCOURAGE ME? The people around us influence our passions. They can build us up and encourage us, or tear us down. Who in your circle is supportive and like-minded? Do they share your passions for life? Do they want to see you succeed in what you care about most deeply, or do they have a silent axe to grind?

5. WHAT MAKES ME HAPPY? Where do you find the most joy? What creates a sense of fulfillment in your mind, body, and soul? Are you doing it? If not, what do you need to clear away so you can achieve the level of happiness you want and deserve?

6. WHO CAN I HELP ON THEIR JOURNEY? Part of the human experience is to connect with and reach others; including helping others to reach their potential and embrace their passions. With whom can you connect and assist on their journey?

MEASURE YOUR PROGRESS. How can you tell when you are embracing your True Self? It's easier than you might think. Quite simply, you feel good... light... open. You are comfortable in your own skin, and everyone knows it and can see it. Your doubts and distractions dissolve, and are replaced by calm and peace. You breathe easy, your body is relaxed, and you make decisions that are confident and full of purpose. If this doesn't describe you, please answer the Six Questions of True Self-Discovery again.

CONSIDERATIONS FOR YOUR TRUE SELF

- Nurture and forgive those who are on your path, but are making mistakes. Forgiveness isn't the same as acceptance. By forgiving, it doesn't mean you accept what they did; it means that what they did has no power over you anymore.

- Don't worry about making mistakes. We *all* make them. Life isn't about achieving perfection. It's about what you learn and how it makes you feel. When it happens and you finally catch on, drop your ego, admit your mistake fully, and make amends. Learn from it so you don't repeat that same lesson again. Then forgive yourself and move on.

- Plan for the future, but live in the moment. Be present... with yourself and with those around you. We live in a hyper-connected world consumed by and with technology. Put your phone down. Logoff. Just *be*... with yourself and with those you love.

- Please laugh—a lot. Life and love are fun, amazing, and full of crazy mischief if you allow it in. Take the time to remember that you are *here*... and that in itself is a blessing.

Whatever you do... wherever you go... whomever you are with... never, *ever* quit your daydream.

ABOUT THE AUTHOR

. . . .

Charles J. Orlando is an interpersonal relations and relationship dynamics researcher who frequently goes undercover in the worlds of dating, marriage and infidelity. His center of study is the intersection where technology and love collide. His writing highlights his real-world experiences that bring to light the issues that plague modern-day relationships. Visit Charles on his website at charlesjorlando.com.

Other Books By Charles J. Orlando

The Problem with Women... is Men®
The Evolution of a Man's Man to a Man of Higher Consciousness

The Problem with Women... is Men®: Volume 2
A Social Media Memoir

For more information, visit charlesjorlando.com